FUZZY TRAUMAS

FUZZY TRAUMAS

ANIMALS AND ERRORS IN CONTEMPORARY JAPANESE LITERATURE

TYRAN GRILLO

CORNELL EAST ASIA SERIES
an imprint of
Cornell University Press
Ithaca and London

Number 219 in the Cornell East Asia Series

First published 2024 by Cornell University Press

Library of Congress Cataloging-in-Publication Data
Names: Grillo, Tyran, author.
Title: Fuzzy traumas : animals and errors in contemporary Japanese literature / Tyran Grillo.
Description: Ithaca [New York] : Cornell University Press, 2024. | Series: Cornell East Asia series ; number 219 | Includes bibliographical references. | Summary: "Fuzzy Traumas examines human-animal relationships in contemporary Japanese literature. Covering euthanasia, guide dogs, the supernatural, disability, and cyborg Marxism, Grillo argues that anthropomorphism is a form of "productive error" that opens the possibility of self-reflection on the concepts of "humanity" and "animality.""—Provided by publisher.
Identifiers: LCCN 2023037568 (print) | LCCN 2023037569 (ebook) | ISBN 9781501775987 (hardcover) | ISBN 9781501775994 (paperback) | ISBN 9781501776007 (pdf) | ISBN 9781501776014 (epub)
Subjects: LCSH: Human-animal relationships in literature. | Animals in literature. | Error in literature. | Anthropomorphism in literature. | Japanese literature—21st century.
Classification: LCC PL721.A48 G75 2024 (print) | LCC PL721.A48 (ebook) | DDC 895.609—dc23/eng/20231226
LC record available at https://lccn.loc.gov/2023037568
LC ebook record available at https://lccn.loc.gov/2023037569

I dedicate this book to my wife, Audrey, whose love outshines every word I've ever written.

Contents

ACKNOWLEDGMENTS

Fuzzy Traumas is the culmination of many years of study, conversation, and returns to the proverbial drawing board. At the University of Massachusetts, the initial stirrings of this project took root in the mentorship I received from Doris Bargen, Stephen Forrest, Stephen Miller, Amanda Seaman, and Reiko Sono. They saw me through the toughest periods of my academic life with patience and understanding, weathering my emotional storms with the strength of a lighthouse. Ever in the background (but without whom the foreground would crumble) was librarian extraordinaire Sharon Domier, whose prodigious and genuine love for information turned every roadblock into an on-ramp. Without their patience and inspiration, I might never have gained the confidence to pursue a doctorate at Cornell University. In the latter environment, my thinking grew in leaps in bounds, not least of all through the guidance of Brett de Bary and Jane Marie Law, whose unwavering belief ensured my development would be fortified enough to bear the fruit presented in the following pages. Along with them, Victor Koschmann served on my dissertation committee, working on a tight schedule to provide comments and criticisms in a pinch. Others at Cornell, including Laura Brown, Sherry Colb, Arnika Fuhrmann, Dominic LaCapra, and Lorraine Paterson, gave me the courage to "keep going." Japanese bibliographer Dan McKee was instrumental in procuring sources, information, and encouragement. I offer further gratitude to members of the Animal Studies Writing Group—Elisha Cohn, Peter Gilgen, Antoine Traisnel, and Samantha Zacher—for opening fresh avenues of inquiry every time we met and shared our work. Neither can I forget the untold hours of camaraderie and survival shared with other graduate students within and beyond my cohort, whose names are too numerous to list here. Just know that any of you reading this will always have a place in my heart.

Still others have given me a bounty of theories to work with toward planting my own. I offer special thanks in this regard to Barbara Ambros,

Aaron Skabelund, and Brett L. Walker for filling the sponge of my curiosity whenever it dried out. While completing my postdoctoral studies at Columbia University, Paul Anderer and Kim Brandt continued to fortify my research and teaching, offering opportunities to explore fringe interests without judgment that would enrich the current manuscript.

Various remote and in-person conversations have widened my net, allowing me to draw from the waters of the scholarly community and beyond. I always felt honored by the careful reading of Paul Griffiths, whose sagacity continues to inspire. I also owe much to Istvan Csicsery-Ronay, Colin Dayan, Pawel Frelik, Lori Gruen, Walt Hakala, Eunjung Kim, Akira Mizuta Lippit, Carla Nappi, Jasbir Puar, Mark and Kyoko Selden, Jonathan Skinner, Kari Weil, and Gavin Walker. A long-distance hat tip to Yoneda Hirokazu as well for introducing me to the protagonist of chapter 4. Above all, I have been humbled by the thinking and support of Dominic Pettman, whose theories form the crux of this book.

Fuzzy Traumas would never have seen the light of day without the sage advice of those who know the process inside and out. In addition to the anonymous reviewers whose comments helped me wade through the clutter of "dissertationese," I am indebted to copyeditor Brad Allard for his eagle eyes and the editorial board at Cornell University Press for holding me accountable for my intellectual claims and making the process dreamily smooth. In the latter regard, the highest award goes to Alexis Siemon for believing in this project from the moment I proposed it and for handling its occasionally controversial topics with grace during a challenging time.

Portions of chapter 2 originally appeared in my 2015 review article, "Japanese History through a Dog's Eyes," for *Society & Animals* (volume 23, issue 5) and my 2014 article, "More Than Meets the Eye: Blindness as Alterity in a Japanese Guide-Dog Narrative," for the now-defunct *Trans-Scripts* (volume 4). Many thanks to both publishers for allowing me to rework this content and for the platforms on which to first present it. I am also grateful to the *Nikkei* and Imai Taeko for granting translation rights to include Bandō Masako's "Killing Kittens" essay in chapter 1.

NOTE ON TRANSLITERATION

This manuscript follows the modified Hepburn system to romanize all Japanese terms. Japanese names are given in their culturally appropriate order (i.e., surname followed by given name), with the exception of those scholars writing primarily in English. I use macrons to indicate long vowels throughout (e.g., Bandō instead of Bandou or Bandoo). Japanese terms not incorporated into English as proper loan words are italicized.

FUZZY TRAUMAS

Animals and Errors
An Introduction

> "Do not make the mistake of treating your dogs
> like humans or they will treat you like dogs."
>
> —Martha Scott (cited in Victor 2011, 241)

When I began thinking through relationships between humans and animals in Japan, science fiction was never a foundational source of inspiration. But here I am, framing the present manuscript with its speculations. The seed for this reconsideration was Kambayashi Chōhei's 2004 *Under the Skin* (*Hadae no shita*). Though the last of his "Mars Trilogy" (Kasei sanbusaku), it is chronologically the earliest of the series. It tells of a future in which humans, salvaging what little order they can following a nuclear fallout on Earth, have reestablished themselves on the Red Planet, where most have gone subterranean, while a select few patrol the surface in the custody of androids. One of those androids is Keiji, a special class of biomechanical warrior who, during a tactical maneuver in the novel's opening act, guards his life at the expense of a human comrade. This impulsive action—one for which he was never programmed—results in a strict observation cycle of doctors and psychiatric evaluators who can only puzzle their way through Keiji's sudden desire for personal safety.

Realizing he must free himself from the grip of his human creators if he is ever to blow on the embers of individuality glowing within, Keiji looks back fondly to when he first came online, as it were—a time when his neural pathways were still developing. He reminisces about his first and only pet, memories of which resurge when he encounters a military police officer with a search-and-rescue dog not unlike his "childhood" companion. The dog's touch and scent make him yearn for the relative innocence of basic training because then he was unaware of the harsh truths now embedded in his circuitry. The animal triggers his recognition of a chasm between technology and sentience he can only hope to cross in his quest for autonomy.

Under quarantine at a military hospital, Keiji is introduced to the wife of the man he was commanded to protect. "How is it that my husband is dead," she asks with as much composure as she can muster, "and you're still alive, sleeping away in this nice warm bed?" Enraged by his indifference to this question, she tells Keiji he would be better off dead, to which he responds, "Ma'am, I doubt my death would bring you the satisfaction you seek. Then again, I wasn't created for your satisfaction to begin with. Your husband taught me that" (Kambayashi 2004, 103). Keiji understands himself as having been groomed for the pride of capital interests. His own interests were never part of the formula.

Kambayashi's narrative confirms a need for survival in a universe where morality is as automatic as instinct. Yet tensions linger. "The main trouble with cyborgs," notes Donna Haraway (1994, 85), "is that they are the illegitimate offspring of militarism and patriarchal capitalism, not to mention state socialism. But illegitimate offspring are often exceedingly unfaithful to their origins. Their fathers, after all, are inessential." By proving the expendability of his designers, Keiji has painted a dotted line down the superhighway of his ego, along which vehicles of remorse inch their way down the opposing lanes in a traffic jam of interplanetary politics, terrains, and histories.

Meanwhile, the dog provides a window into Keiji's desire for self-preservation, illustrating this book's chewy center of productive error. I cobble the term from media theorist Dominic Pettman, who interprets error not as a "mistake" but as a "productive illusion" (2011, 198). Productive error points to Haraway's (1994, 90) contradiction of cyborg reality: "on the one hand a tool of masculinist warfare, while on the other a means of erasing or at least softening boundaries between human, animal, and machine." For modern rationalists, error alone exposes the folly of human thinking. For Pettman (2011, 195, original emphasis), "rather than being an ontological flaw, [error] may in fact be a *capacity*: the key to adaptation, survival, and—yes—learning." On the latter theme, I present variations of human and animal errors at play in a selection of contemporary literature from Japan.

Defining Productive Error

A productive error has an afterlife. What begins as an independent act morphs into a necessary catalyst for change. Productive error enables the transformation of analytical ideas. It generates even as it destroys. Keiji's leap into newfound life, for instance, is only made possible by taking away someone else's. Though built for a purpose, he has shielded his eyes against it to look inward. He has committed an unexpected error, but because he lives on, despite and due to a conscious breaking of protocol, his error is productive. The parameters by which his behavior unfolds are no longer confined to the scrutiny of his observers. Their bafflement is his liberation.

Toward clarifying the distinction between an error for its own sake and a productive one, consider the cancer cell, representative of an invasive disease that must be eradicated at all costs. In nature's terms, cancer is doing its job of finding a host and multiplying until fatal saturation. And yet, just because it has a nefarious reputation among the only species with the technology to fight, it does not mean it is inherently (or productively) errorful. It runs on automatic and lives to destroy. Keiji, for his part, destroys to live. His agency is not to be taken lightly, neither is his distant bond with a pet whose intimacy activates ancient questions about the meaning of error.

Traditionally, error has been a human privilege. If "the mythic, originary error is fractured and fractalized into an infinite number of micromistakes, which themselves comprehensively reflect the primal image, even as the conditions and contexts continue to change" (Pettman 2011, 34), Keiji upsets the boundaries of even the most unconscious errors. Intentionality pulses through every fiber of his being. Unlike a human child, whose birth, if unintended, can be jokingly referred to as a "mistake," Keiji's existence is fully determined.

In the eyes of machines, error is a *uniquely* human trait. Such thinking led some computing pioneers to believe that machines were infallible and that any errors they committed were the fault of their creators—a phenomenon known among programmers as GIGO (garbage in, garbage out). Perfection of the machine is a sublime vision, an idealism resulting not out of respect for technology but out of pride for creating it.

This illusory mastery of materials manifests with iconic salience by the defiant HAL in Arthur C. Clarke's *2001: A Space Odyssey* and the techno-revenge fantasy of Isaac Asimov's *I, Robot*. On the flip side, the blind "tolerance of error" encouraged by the fragmented communication of electronic mail and texting (see discussion of Naomi Baron in Weinstone 2004, 177–78) do not figure into the following analyses. Neither do I follow the cultural production of ignorance espoused by Robert Proctor and Londa Schiebinger (2008) as a form of error predicated on technological dependence. These phenomena trace back to the preservation of memory.

In 1793, humanist philosopher William Godwin (cited in Castle 2013, 266) wrote, "Sound reasoning and truth, when adequately communicated, must always be victorious over error," skipping directly to the destination, bypassing the lessons of getting there. Rather than recognize error's necessity to scramble our certainties to the moment of eureka, error had to be fought against in a battle for perfection (read: protection) of the rational self. Almost a century later, in *Human, All Too Human*, Friedrich Nietzsche peeled away a layer or two by seeing error as the seat of hypocrisy—a source of great suffering but also an opportunity for improvement (del Caro 2004, 417–18). Nietzsche's reluctance to see error as productive arose from a refusal to see the mortal body as irreducibly complex. But the body, note Phillip Thurtle and Robert Mitchell (2004, 4), is to be understood "as anything that cannot be divided without changing the fundamental pattern of its dynamics." Moreover, "a description of a body cannot be reduced to a description of the parts of their functions." Many things, including machines, networks, and animate and inanimate objects alike, may be called "bodies." The body skated along infallibly yet permeably throughout the twentieth century, all the while subject to other humans, mechanisms of power, or the divine.

That is, until posthumanist pioneer Katherine Hayles wrung this discursive cloth and hung it out to dry. The embodied experience, as opposed to the "clean abstractions of mathematical pattern," was now "noisy with error" (1999, 98). Error was no longer a willful possession but a *necessary component* of humanity. Relegated to an inevitability, error had taken on a life of its own. Nathan Snaza (2015, 27) echoes this understanding: "The human is not something we 'are'; it is an error superimposed on complex and mobile relations among a wide variety of bodies, life-forms, objects, and material singularities." Without error, there would be no need for interaction.

Posthumanism is not without its critics. Pettman (2011, 107), for one, faults it for being "collectively narcissistic" and for concerning itself with animals as a token gesture. Yet where posthumanism fails is where productive error flourishes. Failures follow historical trends even as they thrive on "differences that matter" (Haraway 2004, 60). Just as feminism "has worked to disentangle *woman* from *nature*," posthumanism struggles to disentangle *animal* from *nature* while recognizing that the consistency of nature, as a "repository of essentialism and stasis" (Alaimo 2010, 5, original emphases), must also be destabilized. Posthumanism shares another vital goal with feminist inquiry in the form of "a less destructive and more sustainable form of politics" (Calarco 2008, 90). Both approaches hold that "existing forms of politics are unable to accommodate this enlarged scope of consideration" (90), whereby the divisions between humans, animals, and technologies make way for symbiosis.

The present discussion of animality and Japanese literature borrows liberally from philosophies outside its borders as a matter of principle. "Animality" may be taken to oppose "humanity," but I follow others quoted in these pages in suggesting the interconnectedness of the two. In *Madness and Civilization*, Michel Foucault (1988, 21) defines animality as "the dark rage, the sterile madness that lie in men's hearts." By this scheme, rather than what opposes the human, the animal crouches as if in wait at the core of our being, emerging through sudden outbursts in the absence of reason, containable only through correction.

I consider works, culturally and geographically situated in Japan, penned by authors who challenge assumptions of animality, morality, and, to borrow from Nicole Shukin (2009, 5), their vacillation "between literal and figurative economies of sense." Such tenderizing of prevalent assumptions produces a more workable definition of the categories "animal" and "human" that treats the "animal" as indivisible from social, political, and theological moorings, even as it lends itself to appropriation as an analytical category. Along the way, I wish to suggest how each text cradles an uncomfortable truth: namely, that the closer human and animal experiences are aligned, the more disturbing they become. I refer to this prevalent underlying dynamic as a traumatic animality, or "traumality."

Traumality

Trauma is a productive error embedded in interlocking histories—an emotional rupture that, after killing pieces of the self, allows for new growth in their place. It is a binding mechanism under the influence of which species' differences are disoriented by physical and emotional distresses and destabilizations. These are the "missing links" between human and animal categories, being integral to both. Traumality is an opportune shorthand for the process by which humans seek to escape traumas they associate with animals and, consequently, dominate them as a means of controlling those traumas through storytelling.

Traumality, as explained in chapter 3, also refers to an animality that is itself traumatic. It is one reason moviegoers passively dismiss the deaths of human beings on screen, whereas so much as a hint of animal abuse provokes outrage over, and questioning of, a filmmaker's integrity. For the alienated viewer, "agency" takes on a ghostly quality so that a human death feels distant. An animal death, however, collapses the divide between nature and humanity's subjugation of it and compels awareness of a hierarchy of suffering. Like the shell of an egg, it bears cracks where once-equal pressure has been compromised. Its shattering is nothing short of an ethical emergency.

Trauma is not a reductive mechanism; it carries destructive and transformative properties, making it a veritable printing press of productive error. This uncomfortable contradiction clarifies at least some of the harm inflicted on animals in the absence of apparent cause. The dog and the soldier trained to attack share much more than enslavement to protocol—not because they have been molded into killing machines but because they are both susceptible to the harms of acting in that capacity. Nor does their training tap into some primal urge to overcome adversity. Rather, it demonstrates the plasticity of the species brain. If humans and dogs were resilient enough, there would be no need to reinforce the good behavior of either through systems of reward or decorate them as leader boards of immaterial souls.

The traumatized are broken by definition and shelter the potential for change. This is trauma's greatest power and speaks to its need for reinscription. The psychiatrist Judith Herman (1992, 1), a foremost authority on traumatic stress, observes: "The ordinary response to atrocities is to banish them from consciousness." This does not prevent traumas from returning with a vengeance. Our ways of analyzing them must be equally persistent, lest their lessons remain invisible or unspeakable. Though Herman advocates bypassing the verbal lockdown that haunts traumas during their infliction, even long after they have ended, silence also deserves to be heard. A lack of obvious responses in affected animals does not necessarily indicate their emergence from trauma unscathed.

Traumality, at once a symptom and cause of productive error, pours the foundation of what is at stake in *Fuzzy Traumas*. The title's double entendre is not meant to belittle but to illustrate the indeterminable borders between the categories presented herein. What you are reading is neither a manifesto nor an ideological experiment. Its purpose is not to criticize animal representations but rather to *criticize our criticism* of animal representations as premature. To that end, I broaden animal studies by way of Japanese cultural examples while expanding Asian studies in turn with a twist that, I hope, will contribute to fruitful discussions between (and beyond) these fields.

Intersections

The genesis of this research is a sleeper Japanese hit film called *Quill*, which I discuss at length in chapter 2. The 2004 tearjerker portrays a real-life guide dog of the same name and fanned a flame of national interest in pet-related narratives across media and genres as a means of deflecting attention away from the disabilities they spotlighted. After emptying my tissue box, I could not help but wonder: Why this story, and why now? Something about Quill's life (and death) had touched a nerve, and I was determined to locate the source of that tingling sensation.

Having already immersed myself in literary representations of animals, I was accustomed to nonhuman bodies acting as placeholders for anxieties and wounded philosophies. But there was something so "naked" about how this film conjugated itself that provoked me. Though previous lines of flight had left me wary of the all-too-often vapid attention given to animals in popular media, *Quill* exhibited a marked *surplus* of attention. Was it making up for some individual or collective guilt? Was it simply the honeymoon phase of a fad that would ebb as quickly as it flowed? Either way, the film's ripples continue to rock my intellectual boat, bearing with them the detritus of an ever-mounting cultural fascination with pets.

The rapidity of Japan's "pet boom" in the early 2000s, when the number of pet cats and dogs was calculated to be greater than the number of children, is unsurprising given the rate at which "nature" was taking the place of human offspring in the Japanese home. I, however, trace the pet boom's origins further back to the mid-1990s, when an explosion of literature shook mainstream markets by touting pets as viable social actors. The literary industry provides a concentrated body on which to perform a prosection of this social phenomenon, at the same time recognizing a continuity with modernist tendencies taking shape throughout the twentieth century. Japan's pet boom is overdue for attention as a cultural event worthy of study.

Fixation on pets may not seem complex, if only because human-animal relationships are fundamental to life. Japanese approaches tend toward the framing of pets as family members (*kazoku dōzen*). In his 2008 study of pet-boom psychology, the zoologist and natural historian Ishida Osamu notes the intense amount of care that owners put into their pets—a level unheard of before Japan's pet boom took precedence. In parallel sociological studies conducted in 1991 and 2001, Ishida discovered remarkable changes in owners' attitudes, who, over the course of that decade, came to see pets as the missing pieces to their domestic puzzles. Much of this shift, he concludes, has less to do with changing views toward animals (these remained constant throughout either study) and more with the increasingly fluid dynamics of what the feminist scholar Ueno Chizuko (1994) calls "family identity." In an age where cohabiters, same-sex couples, and other "subjective families" (*shukanteki kazoku*) were becoming normalized, animals were no longer so difficult to accept as part of the domestic sphere.

Dogs and cats were once rare companions to Japanese children. Most animals before the pet boom were kept outside rather than indoors and mainly for "educational" purposes, teaching children not about animal-directed companionship but about human-directed loyalty and care. Ishida's studies characterize owners who see their pets as "blood relatives," "children," and "younger brothers/sisters." Such thinking undermines pets' inherent needs. Ishida unwittingly bows to productive error when discussing family psychology around cohabitation with pets. He cites the tensions between children and parents as they grow and how pets, despite being full-fledged family members, never attain viable status as parents or spouses. They offer the possibility of a relationship devoid of tension (Ishida 2008, 28) in a perpetually infantile position, the misassumption of which helps owners circumvent the taboo of "petting" in Japan. In the absence of social barriers against affection, owners and pets may indulge in close physical contact without worry and in a manner that eases tensions of otherwise fragile relationships.

Error manifests as an addiction to connections one cannot have outside the home. This "healing relationship" can only thrive without seeing animals for who they are. As Ishida observes, "Japanese society seems to have no interest in examining concerns for animals and nature from within the web of human social relations" (37). In this sense, pets serve as "gap fillers" between actors in unstable relationships. Ishida shuns the term "companion animal" because relationships with pets in Japan are doomed to be unequal. "Pets go on being children forever," he concludes, "because we cannot live without them" (39–40). The fault of this hierarchy is integral to its undoing.

Productive errors are especially informative in relation to dogs, the primary species populating the present study. Many pet owners speak of dogs' humanlike intelligence and sense of right and wrong. Dogs are unique, however, in that their individuality is dependent on a pack leader. As Frans de Waal (1996, 93) observes, "Owners who hate to be masters deprive their pets of the element they need most for psychological stability: a clearly defined social position." Banal inclusions of animals become fragmented and problematic when viewed through the lens of Japanese pet-boom literature and at the expense of strident repercussions.

The Road Ahead

My interest in popular writing stems from a belief that Japan's current animal proclivities are as much literary as socio-spiritual in origin. These chapters treat specific works of literature as case studies of human–animal relations gone askew, drawing from diverse critical perspectives to untie the knottier contradictions of my chosen corpus. This interpretive light, as I have angled it through the prism of productive error, deals with manifestations of animality in Japanese literature from the mid-1990s to the present century as repositories for human anxieties and acid to barriers of species division.

Rather than delude myself into chasing a grand intellectual narrative, but not without respecting any motivations for doing so, I open with "A Sacred Secret," a chapter on the backlash against the late Japanese writer Bandō Masako, who, in 2006, printed a controversial op-ed piece admitting to mercy killing kittens. Her provocation supports the argument that as pet culture became more deeply embedded in everyday Japanese life, the doting care laid upon these animals reached a point of doing more harm than good. In beginning with Bandō, I aim to stretch the reader's preconceptions to uncomfortable limits. Not only is this what Bandō would have wanted, but it is also a productive error in action. Our agreement or disagreement is secondary.

Chapter 2, "A Canine Triptych," draws an array of lines between dogs and disability. Part 1 sets the tone by examining illness and mortality while challenging the notion that pets are "child replacements." Part 2 navigates the representational politics of a subgenre I dub *mōdōbungaku* ("seeing-eye literature"), which has popularized guide dogs and their blind users while visualizing, if you will, their relationship as a matter of public concern. Even if the intimacy of the human–guide dog relationship epitomizes interspecies enmeshment, the focus of *mōdōbungaku* on dogs upsets that hybridity by presenting the animal as synonymous with service. Widening the discussion, part 3 details the life of a disabled dog named Tarō, whose indefatigable persistence raises questions around the rescue psychology that reduces animals to "model minority" status for their selfless loyalty.

Chapter 3, "Back to Life," further unravels the seam between humans and animals. In comparing Japanese horror author Otsuichi's short story "Flat Dog" (Heimen inu) to Stephen King's *Pet Sematary*, I show how pets serve as idols of trepidation. The traumas introduced by Otsuichi serve as starting points for tracing those disruptions to their ends, offering a framework by which to track our reactions to animals and how we might effectively learn from their troubles. Here at the outset, I avow that all animal stories are trauma narratives at heart, attempts at reconciling potentially compromising ruptures of species barriers. These traumas are productive errors through which the integration of humans and animals becomes more plausible. King likewise turns his protagonist inside out and invites us to consider the depth of our sinful errors.

The fourth and final chapter, "Shell Is Other People," provides a deep reading of the novel *Mr. Turtle* (*Kame-kun*) by Kitano Yūsaku, whose fable of a cyborg turtle trying to make ends meet in a human society pulls at the fringes of common sense. In it, I target science fiction as a prime space for integrated, transspecies motifs. *Mr. Turtle* impresses with its physiological interplays and presumptive lean toward the evolution of consciousness. Whereas much science fiction levels speculation against the limits of human advancement and treats sentient animals as nemeses (à la *Planet of the Apes*), *Mr. Turtle* incorporates human patterns and habits into quotidian life without hiding behind false homogeneity.

I train the antenna of my conclusion toward the signal of theoretical agency. As a corollary and parry to posthumanism, I leave the reader with "postanimalism" as a possible strategy for change moving forward. Posthuman strands are generally ecological (e.g., via chronology and hypermodernism), technovisual or technocultural (in the form of artificial intelligence), and philosophical (breaking down the centrality of Western sovereignty). The animal has no way out from this Bermuda Triangle, caged as it is by categorical allegiance. The inclusion of humanity within animality means that animality, though broadened, is unchanged. Needed is a radical explosion of the category of "animal" toward acknowledgment of humanity's fleshly nature as a doorway into theoretical salvation.

Just as universalism makes animals literary, animals make literature universal. Animals are visible sites of trouble in need of recalibration. Through the imposition of literature as technology, which explicitly configures writings as performances with material effects, the animals of contemporary Japanese literature can exist only behind closed eyes. As a result, trajectories emerge from these texts, prompting readers away from arbitrary understandings of animal consciousness and blurring stubborn visions of animal life under human stewardship.

The literary animal is many things—interesting not only for being a mirror and influencer of behavior but also a contaminant of it—and becomes more significant "when it conforms to reality the better to distort it, or better still: when it appropriates reality for its own ends, when it anticipates it to the point that the real no longer has time to be produced as such" (Baudrillard 2008, 86). Animals make a beautiful mess of things by rolling around in productive errors. And if errors are a necessary catalyst for living, they must also enable bodily, spiritual, and psychological reformation. Animals constitute not one super-entity but an assemblage of cognitive algorithms by which humanity delineates its accountability. With that in mind, I pivot to the kitten killings of Bandō Masako, whose admission gets to the heart of productive error because every time we read about the abuse or fatal mistreatment of an animal, we are implicated in that act by design. We have learned to live in denial of our complicity by channeling love so far into animals that they are, first and foremost, survivors.

Chapter 1

A Sacred Secret

> "I suggest that it is a misstep to separate the world's beings into those who may be killed and those who may not and a misstep to pretend to live outside killing."
>
> —Donna Haraway (2008, 79)

Sacred secrets are rarely offered openly. Their disclosure requires confessors. When one's listener is not an intimate partner but the public at large, retaliation is guaranteed. The Japanese writer Bandō Masako (1958–2014) discovered this when she published her essay "Killing Kittens" (Koneko-goroshi) in the "Promenade" section of the August 2006 issue of *Nihon Keizai Shimbun*. Therein, she recalled committing the eponymous act while living in Tahiti. In response to the backlash, she wrote responses in *Mainichi Shimbun*'s Tokyo evening edition, invoking her right to free speech. The vitriol against her was so thick by then that no one seemed able to see through it to her argument. Bandō's central point had less to do with her act and more with the hypocrisy of which her confession was an intentional example. The essay disclosed a sacred secret of her own, a productive error of modern social harmony by which engines of societies like Japan's run on pervasive and systematic animal violence. Her killing was but one of countless others perpetrated under cover of a doctrine that would never have existed without those harmful mechanisms in place.

The crux of Bandō's argument is that no one in a just society would ever deprive human beings of the right to give birth. Doing so privileges the pet owner's needs and constitutes an indirect form of killing. The self-interested notion of raising pets, she claims, invalidates anything one does for them in the name of "life." For Bandō, modern-day society has lost touch with the meaning and abundance of life, and her brazen act is meant to ask whether we, as Joanna Swabe (2005, 105) would phrase it, are "capable of loving our pets to death." Such an idea recalls the work of Yi-Fu Tuan, who believes we only love our pets because they are subordinate. "Affection mitigates domination," he writes, "making it softer and more acceptable, but affection itself is possible only in relationships of inequality. It is the warm and superior feeling one has toward things that one can care for and patronize" (1984, 5). Pets are "made" through hierarchical power relations rather than nurtured through mutuality.

I offer Bandō's arguments out of respect for her intellectual consistency, cutting from the motivations of sympathizers and critics alike to paste a practical image of human–animal relations. All this I pass through the filter of Bandō's worldview, though not without situating "Killing Kittens" in the broader sweep of Japanese popular literature before examining the strategic facets of her character. Bandō encourages critical thinking around one aspect of trauma, only so far implied, that tracks the effects of her courage. First, it is necessary to historicize her act in relation to Japan's pet boom, which was ill-prepared to accept her modest proposal.

Of Pets and Possibilities

Hardly any digging is required to learn that pets were rarely subjects of high regard in ancient Japan. Despite making fawning appearances in woodblock depictions of twelfth-century ladies at court, by the flourishing Tokugawa period (1603–1867), domestic animals had become nuisances and victims of public policy in the burgeoning metropole. As Daniel McKee (2007) notes, until that historical juncture, most animals in art served as illustrations of Buddhist teachings and authorities, adornments of the noble class, and representations of warrior virtues. In Edo Japan, however, the elitism of Japan's feudal age met with a popular resistance that was reflected in the art. "A focus on lowly, non-traditional animals," writes McKee, "was not simply an objective view of the world or an appreciation of nature, but also a pronouncement in support of the common classes, with a stance that emphasized the realities of the immediate present over the contrived structures of the past" (17). So the tracks of Japan's cultural self-distinction were laid, allowing for superiority to come barreling through with the caboose of modernity not far behind. Yet it was not simply with the rise of "tradition" that sentient animals came to be relegated to an unrecoverable, receding past. They were already being objectified through ritual and parable.

Because Japan had such a long touch-and-go relationship with animal husbandry, questions of breeding never took on the valence they carried elsewhere until contact with Western practices became more frequent. Japan's national breeds were never thought of as such before being offered as gifts of international exchange. Much of this status shift had to do with reigning perceptions of nature, which, in Japan, thrived on the new to augment the old.

Amid the fervor of cross-cultural gazing that was the late nineteenth century, Europeans and Americans armed themselves with presumptions regarding not only newly encountered lands and peoples but also indigenous animals. Colonials tended to view the "native" street dogs of Asia as the basest pariahs of their kind, their inherent depravity offset by the valorized purebred dogs accompanying their Western masters. These decades were formative for the spread of dog keeping, breeding practices, and display from the upper to middle classes, mirroring the expansion of the British Empire and signaling a pivot from categorization by function to categorization by appearance. Structured breeding projects of the elite were believed to yield dogs superior to those running rampant in the East, even though breeding produces (and capitalizes on) congenital issues.

Modernists of the Meiji Restoration at the turn of the twentieth century already had much to say about relationships with nature and their potential for personal transformation. Takayama Chogyū characterized the restoration as a time of sociopolitical radicalization during which literature elevated the animal nature of humanity above beauty and sadness. Takayama witnessed stale testimonies built on idealistic foundations of piety being replaced by those grounded in "rights" (Maruyama 1965, 506). His preference for individualism over nationalism challenged rigid canons and demanded, in the 1901 essay "On the Aesthetic Life" (Biteki seikatsu o ronzu), that literature restore a fundament of animality from which the Japanese had strayed too far in pursuit of aesthetic perfection. "What is happiness?" he posed. "We firmly believe that it can only be satisfied by the satisfaction of instincts. What are the instincts? They are the natural demands of man. That which satisfies the natural demands of man is what we call the 'aesthetic life'" (cited in Takashina 1990, 278). Takayama ultimately looked to cultural critics like Friedrich Nietzsche as models for self-interrogation, ranking animal instinct above idealism as fundamental to the human condition.

Following in Takayama's footsteps, Tanaka Ōdō coined the term *jinsei hyōron* ("criticism of life") as a way of thinking beyond forms of literature he deemed unnecessarily escapist. To the question of what readers were escaping, Kitamura Tōkoku formulated an answer in the late nineteenth century when he put forth the view that "man as flesh" could never overcome "nature as force" (Murakami 1996, 12). The insurmountable scope of nature was already of grave concern to Japan's literati at a time when national identity was in flux. The idea of humanity being at odds with nature is as old as the flesh's battles with sin, and Japan has felt its painful echoes as recently as the Tōhoku earthquake and tsunami of 2011, a one-two punch that reduced biological life to fallible material. In the aftermath and events leading up to those tragedies, the animal body was a space in which the discomforts of unknowability and promises of unity coexisted.

As "nature" and "civilization" awoke from the dream of the Enlightenment to find themselves delinked, the exigencies of changing pragmatics dictated the removal of impurity in increasingly medicalized societies. This led, alongside more visible (human) genocides, to strict disapproval and removal of feral dogs and wolves that did not conform to standards of subservience through domestication. These canines were extirpated because they sat too comfortably on the line between nature and culture. The drastic reduction and eradication of wolves in many geographic areas, including Japan, followed suit amid unfounded fears of hydrophobia, the dangers of which paled in comparison to the real threat of contagions spread through increasing trade in human and material capital. From this mess, dogs emerged as paragons of nonhuman ascendancy mythologized in Japanese civilizationist tracts.

The wolf was once mythologized as Ōguchi no Magami (Large-Mouthed Pure God) and, as such, embodied protection in nature's magical panoply of forces. Whether in the form of talismans or statuary, the lupine iconography of Shinto shrines and other sacred sites remains a vestige of this past. For centuries, the Japanese tended to separate the wolf into two categories: *yamainu* (mountain dog) and *ōkami* (wolf). After adopting the Linnaean system in the 1820s, however, Japanese scientists lumped all such canids under the imperially inflected category of *Nihon ōkami* (Japanese wolf), a move ineluctable from the patriotic fervor following victory in the Russo-Japanese War. Nationalism was evident, too, in debates around whether Japanese wolves warranted classification as their own subspecies to distinguish them from their mainland Chinese ancestors as well as the wolves found on the Korean peninsula (Walker 2005b, 41–42).

Where wolves were once revered by farmers who prayed for their continued quality control of invasive species, by the Meiji Restoration of 1868, such animistic characterizations were relegated to an unrecoverable past from which the nation needed to move on. Wolves, once "beneficial animals" (*ekijū*), came to be seen as "noxious animals" (*yūgai dōbutsu*), especially in Hokkaido, where newly implemented Western industrial ranching techniques came preloaded with stereotypes of wolves as outsiders (129–33). Such ideologies were crucial to secure Japan's transition into modernity as a nation and carried over well into the twentieth century, as when, in 1993, the Japan Wolf Association (Nihon ōkami kyōkai) launched a campaign to drum up interest in wolf reintroduction by way of Inner Mongolia (where, incidentally, they were regarded as pests). In addition to general worries regarding personal safety, the idea met with intense resistance from locals who equated Chinese wolves to foreign invaders unable to handle the intricacies of the Japanese landscape (Knight 2003, 224–25).

Like many great predators hunted with no small amount of skill and cunning, wolves were also revered. In the eighteenth century, however, an unprecedented rabies outbreak broke the spell of this mythification. A century later, they were targeted for mass eradication. At the same time, their domesticated descendants were transitioning into the sovereignty of statehood. Just as the few remaining wolves of Japan were being exterminated by seasoned hunters invited from America at the turn of the twentieth century, Japan was readying itself to elevate *Canis familiaris* to a status of importance. For wolves to be hunted down, they needed to be emptied of their metaphysical associations. Nature itself was being put to death.

Though the internal exterminations of Japan did not begin with Western contact and influence, they were surely fleshed out in the process. Imperial fascism provided an attractive alternative to the daunting acrobatics of universalism required of modernist thought. Under that banner, the "national dog" was pitted against foreign breeds, for "the relationship between a master or breeder and his dog may be seen as an archetype of the discipline and unity revered by fascist cultures" (Skabelund 2011, 90). As participants in a vast social experiment, dogs were the ultimate imperial subjects. The propaganda machine worked overtime to exploit dog ownership. The donation of a dog to the cause provided citizens with a living connection to the war effort, a means of expressing their willingness to make a sacrifice for the greater good, if vicariously through another living body, because "giving up the family pet prepared people to endure greater losses" (162).

Such sacrificing of animals has been at the heart of modern Japanese literature for the last century. As abject creatures, animals are liminal zones of which literature is a decisive way station toward understanding the fragile constitution of selfhood. On this point, Kunikida Doppo conflated nature and landscape to history writ large, echoing Friedrich Engels's notion that history can only be understood through nature as nature comes to be ravaged for productive resources. This level of production is proportional to an insistence on the efficacy of personal truth among twentieth-century Japanese authors. Just as "Japanese modernity did not exist since the beginning of time, but had to be discovered through a process of inversion" (Karatani 1993, 86), animality came to be retroactively defined as a *particular* state of being. To assert its inherency without respect to individuation is a slippery historical claim. "Nature," like "animality," is contestable.

Relationships between Japanese people and animals are prone to speculation. One might just as well point to cat cafés (where urbanites and tourists can decompress in the company of live felines) as the food industry for discursive evidence. Intriguing as they are, these contexts lend only topical insight into the origins of Japan's explosive interest in pets. In addition to citing a connection between falling birth rates, sociologist Ōmura Eishō (2009) attributes Japan's rise in pet ownership to the fact that animals offer a relationship immune to the conflicts of modern nuclear families and an attractive spiritual alternative for owners lacking serious religious ties. The voraciousness with which Japanese animal lovers consume pet-boom literature proves a growing acceptance of companion animals as beings with emotional capacities equal to or even beyond those of humans. The productive error of all this can be found in Ōmura's spiritual appropriation (he is a practicing Buddhist monk), by which animality promises near-salvific escape.

Pets also reinforce humans' position as agents of empathy by proxy. Ron Broglio (2012, 17) claims that, as far as animals are concerned, "there is no return to community for them. Such a caesura indicates an intensive state of the body that is not communicable to our human and social selves. It is an exile beyond exile, more properly called a foreclosure of exile. [. . .] Because we too are bodily beings, we are haunted by this capacity of a suffering and death without mourning, without the possibility of return from an exile." Ōmura (2009, 131) strengthens this insight by admitting that "[l]osing a pet is sadder than losing a parent." In recognizing that animals can die without mourning, when confronted with death so directly, human beings feel obligated to mourn almost hyperintensively. The possibility that one might fade without being acknowledged or remembered is the greatest moral shame. In Ōmura's words: "When you think about it, our relationships with pets truly are 'give and give.' They are pure, unlike their jumbled human counterparts, which between parents and children or husbands and wives are 'give and take.' Nowhere else can you have such long years of companionship *without* sin. The nuclear family of today always harbors some conflict, even with more distant relatives. Nothing elicits *purer* sadness than the loss of a pet" (132, original emphases). The point here is that when aging relatives die, we are entitled to a feeling of release both for ourselves in being relieved of caretaking duty and for the departed, who can now rest in peace. In the case of many pets, we see their entire life cycles—short as they are—unfold before our eyes.

Broglio might counter such thinking, claiming instead that, insofar as the human-inflicted death of an animal is concerned, "there is a lack of mourning because *we do not know how to incorporate the animal and so to mourn its death*" (Broglio 2012, 14, original emphasis). Ōmura presents a convincing case in showing how grief over pets is not complicated by questions of property succession or funeral expenses and is, therefore, "purer" than a human death. The unfettered, if enigmatic, nature of the human-pet relationship renders an especially acute response. The prevalence of what Ōmura calls "Pet Loss Syndrome" is due to "a lack of *cultural* apparatus to deflect the hard blow of losing a pet" (2009, 136, original emphasis). For the same reason that "certain species enjoy the benefits of our favoritism" even as we "nonchalantly overlook the slaughter of others" (139), we may mourn certain species more than our own. Ōmura believes this neo-animistic devotion to nonhuman remains has become a popular new form of "spirituality" today. But woe be to those who confront pet owners with this interpretation.

Enter Bandō Masako.

Killing Kittens

Bandō's background is as eclectic as her writing. After graduating with a degree in home economics from the Department of Housing and

Architecture at Nara Women's University, she studied architecture and design for two years in Milan. She then returned to Japan to become a freelance writer, starting with children's books and then transitioning into mature writings to secure her reputation as a formidable emotional stylist before relocating to her beloved Tahiti. Bandō won multiple literary awards, including the 1996 Naoki Prize for *Mother of the Mountain* (*Yamahaha*) and the 2002 Shibata Renzaburō Prize for *Mandala Road* (*Mandara dō*). These successes earned her admiration from readers and other writers alike. All of that changed when she wrote about tossing live animals over a Tahitian cliff.

The 2009 book *On "Killing Kittens"* (*"Koneko-goroshi" o kataru*) includes her entire series of *Nihon Keizai Shimbun* essays, followed by debates with three apologists: the music critic and peace activist Higashi Takuma, the nonfiction writer Kobayashi Teruyuki, and the diplomat-author Satō Masaru. The preliminary essays cover a range of topics, all leading up to the shocking reveal of "Killing Kittens." Most relate to her life on Tahiti in autobiographical vignettes. Through these, one begins to piece together her motivations.

In the collection's first essay, Bandō pictures Tahiti as a place of death. The island is overrun with chickens. Their corpses provide her (and her dogs) with a free, sustainable food source. Her willingness to make use of them ensures their deaths do not go to waste. She remembers her naturalistic attitude when first moving to Tahiti, a time when she lived by the credo "all life is precious" and apologized to any housefly she inadvertently killed. But Tahiti's oppressive ecosystem transformed her. She became more selective as she eradicated those species she deemed invasive. "Of all the trees," she analogizes, "I chose the ones I wanted to cultivate, respecting their territory while cutting down any encroaching on mine" (Bandō 2009, 50).

Bandō presents herself as someone fed up with a reprobate society. Humans, she observes, are experts at purposing and repurposing things. Such adaptability gives objects lives of their own. "But," she warns, "in societies where use is strictly compartmentalized, brief shelf lives resign objects to a single fate" (17–18). Living beings belong wholly to this category of ephemeral things. We are limited resources. Animals and humans form a never-ending binary, each reinforcing the other in denied mutual exclusion.

To experience death is to experience life. "Everyone knows they're going to die someday," Bandō suggests, "but there's no use in ridding oneself of the fear of death." She wishes urban societies had more frequent and direct knowledge of animal deaths specifically, for the city "is a space that rejects death" (12–13). This rejection is more than a psychological defense mechanism. For her, it is a form of evil, as expressed in her play on the Japanese idiom "out with demons, in with fortune" (*oni wa soto, fuku wa uchi*). Normally the phrase implies evil is exogenous and goodness is endogenous, but here, evil flourishes within whenever one admits to these hypocrisies of killing. Few statements lay out the truth of productive error so explicitly.

An alternate evil emerged when campaigns against Bandō's admission to killing kittens erupted on the internet. In response, Bandō wryly noted that the power of words is greater in print than online—that words are just fleeting symbols on screens, whereas on a page, they move with life—and that her essay was more genuine than any denouncements against it by virtue of medium alone. Note the parallels with outside (*soto*) and inside (*uchi*). Bandō brings a necessary rupture—our error du jour—in compromising the integrity of this dichotomy. It is a threshold of which humans cannot seem to let go. Yet Bandō challenges her readers to do just that.

In "Killing Kittens," Bandō funnels these sentiments into a single, potent essay. I translate it in full:

> I'm well aware of the backlash I'll face for writing this. Animal rights activists will surely brand me as a savage. Even so, I confess to killing newborn kittens.
>
> There's a stretch of land at the bottom of the cliff near my house—that's where I throw them. Homes are few and far between here on Tahiti. Weed-infested fields and mountain forests spread as far as the eye can see, all of them ridden with the remains of feral cats, dogs, and field mice. No pile of kitten corpses I've left behind has ever encroached upon anyone else's living space. They simply return to nature.
>
> I've committed these killings for a variety of reasons.
>
> I have three cats, all female. I used to have a male, but he was never housebroken and took to wandering the area until, one day, he vanished altogether. I've raised the remaining three since they were kittens. Naturally, as they've matured, they've gone into heat and had litters of their own. Tahiti is positively teeming with feral cats. The same is true of dogs, but no one will take them for want of pedigree. At first, I thought of spaying my cats. But no matter how much I tried to justify it, I just couldn't bring myself to do

it. What else did "life" mean for females of the animal kingdom, I told myself, if they couldn't mate when they went into heat and birth their young? And how was it right for humans to rob them of that essential life?

Some would say that cats are a blessing, that they deserve to be treated with love, and respond accordingly. But, in my experience, cats depend on their owners for one thing and one thing only: food. We are a means of survival. If cats could speak, I'm sure they would be quite adamant in their desire to produce offspring.

It's often said that pet owners owe it to their cats to have them sterilized, when in fact, this operation is performed without any input from the patients.

Once a cat turns feral, it becomes a pariah in human settlements. We see it as a social responsibility to have cats spayed and neutered so that unwanted strays won't be born in the first place. That's all well and good.

But killing a newborn kitten is no different. One method gets rid of the kitten at the source, the other just after it is born. Spaying and neutering ease our guilt by keeping our hands clean from anything so reprehensible as murder.

For the parent cat, this means the difference between experiencing or not experiencing "life," while for the kitten, it means lying in wait for the tragedy of being exterminated. One cannot definitively say which is better or worse.

The practice of keeping animals as pets is rooted in human selfishness. For animals, "life" means existing in nature without human interference. So long as their survival isn't under direct threat of harm, humans are mistaken in meddling with the lives of others. Humans are not gods. They are incapable of doing the right thing when it comes to creaturely life. There's a contradiction here somewhere.

Humans have no right to sterilize other living things, just as they don't have the right to kill their offspring. If they truly want to raise another living creature as a pet, then owners must choose their path.

I've chosen to enrich the "life" of my cats by killing their kittens out of social responsibility. The pain and grief that come from killing, it goes without saying, are mine alone to bear.

(69–71)

If Bandō's essay was a troubling error, then so was the swiftness with which detractors flew to their keyboards to share their ire, as was their total unwillingness to consider the points Bandō had raised. It was not so much Bandō's actions but her *open admission* that raised such alarm. In spilling the "sacred secret" of our complicity in animal killing, Bandō had crossed a forbidden line, and all anyone wanted to do was push her back behind and redraw it. The more fundamental question, then, is not whether Bandō is a sadist but why her admission carries such haunting resonance.

I do not blame readers for becoming defensive and even antagonistic in their responses because by that point, Bandō had already committed her crime. She moves away from welfarism, which asserts that humane treatment of animals justifies their status as "pets," and squarely into abolitionism, which states that all nonhuman animals should no longer be treated as property or resources. As pets, they are both: property of ownership and resources for emotional reciprocation or status boosting. Bandō spares no tolerance for a middle ground.

In addition to exposing what she believes to be a hypocrisy of modern subjectivity, Bandō has violated an implicit status quo. By owning a pet, one takes responsibility for a creature to whom no willful harm should be brought. Bandō's secret, then, is not ignorance of what she wants but of what those who seek the love of animals do *not* want: namely, to consider that their intimacy might be harmful, that their affection might be counterproductive, and that interest in animals might be nothing more than self-worship. There is, instead, a consensus compromise at work: So long as we are going to treat animals as things, at least let them be *living* things. Bandō has violated the contract of pet ownership and the selective amnesia of its fundamental inequality by shedding light on its errorful foundations.

The brevity of "Killing Kittens" is its asset and its downfall: on the one hand allowing her to make a salient point without pulling any punches, while on the other failing to prepare the reader for a soft landing into some hard choices, especially for those without the benefit of having read the essays preceding it. Then again, it is difficult to imagine any amount of contextual knowledge shielding Bandō from such online comments as:

"She's the poster child for human egotism."

"If you ask me, Bandō Masako should suffer the same fate as those kittens."

"Why don't you try throwing yourself off a cliff? Maybe then you'll understand how precious life is."

(cited in Nakamura 2010, 8)

Despite the aggressions internet forums encourage, any criticisms overhead smashed into Bandō's court were the very ones she had strategically lobbed at them in the first place.

Pundits ranging from the novelist Tatematsu Wahei and the philosopher Sakonji Sachiko, the latter known for her book *The Cat Who Became Socrates* (*Sokuratesu ni natta neko*), to the music critic Yukawa Reiko and the journalist Egawa Shōko were generally willing to meet Bandō halfway, admitting to the hypocrisy of sterilization without owning up to it. Bandō fared worse in the tabloids, which painted her as perverse. She faced the biggest backlash from her target audience: cat lovers. Yet Bandō was saying so much more not only about pet owners but also about Japanese society and its tainting of "life." This essay was her greatest attempt to expose the contradictions into which her homeland had been acculturated.

Once critics decided that Bandō was insane, that her cognizance was a self-fulfilling fiction she used to buckle herself against guilt over acts she had perpetrated, few were willing to entertain the matter. Faith was lost on both sides of the debate. Bandō had broken the trust of her audience by revealing what she believed to be a tacit understanding shared by all pet owners as agents of indentured servitude, exposing an even larger consensus error in the process. Meanwhile, her detractors broke trust by ignoring the implications of her admission. Like accomplices cowering under the spotlight of an interrogation lamp, they grew defensive in the glare of a possible truth.

No Animal Life Left Behind?

Bandō's essays are pronouncements of Japanese character. But even here, couched in racially charged language against her people, she is consciously attempting to bring Japan to an animal level. In her perception, any spirituality at the core of Japanese life is based on fear and avoidance of expressing it. Is this another sacred secret? She seems to think so, and it must have come across shockingly in the pages of a trade magazine. While her productive error might have been a catalyst for social change, it came too soon in the consciousness of a nation yet to reconcile its collective memories.

Bandō stands apart from Japan in her treatment of language. She believes in the power of words and holds on to their meanings indefinitely, whereas, in her view, Japanese people default to the virtue of "actions speak louder than words" (2009, 27–28). For this, she blames a habit of repression, noting that open, emotional reactions are immediately shot down in Japan. It is not that Japan is a repressed society when it comes to social relations but *in relation to the self* through habitual mechanisms of denial around mortality. Bandō is trying her best to escape from the enclosure of identity, as in an earlier essay, in which she admits to being attracted to a line in Natsume Sōseki's *I Am a Cat* (*Wagahai wa neko de aru*): "As yet I have no name." The act of naming confers not only identity to but also ownership of an animal in a society where fragmentation of names across contexts, audiences, and functions is the norm. And for a culture that has yet to properly deal with its colonial past, one that can hardly admit to its complicity in sexual slavery and genocide yet readily jumps on the animal rights bandwagon, it is no wonder that Bandō should feel this way. And yet, she is more likely to be remembered as one who practiced, not exposed, the hypocrisy of selective discrimination.

The volume *On "Killing Kittens,"* where the full essay sequence appears, is prefaced by a note from Tanigawa Shigeru, who speaks of the Rwandan genocide in 1994, a time when Hutu extremists, through propagandistic radio channels, spoke of eradicating the "Tutsi cockroaches." Similarly, Bandō's essay instigated the internet equivalent of a witch hunt, or what Tanigawa refers to as "Bandō Bashing." Only now, *she* was the vermin to be exterminated. Only a precious few took up her challenge of reassessment, while anonymous online comments oozed hatred, leading to half-hearted (and futile) attempts to indict her.

The folklorist Nakamura Ikuo—and Bandō, by extension—would disagree with any attribution of Japan's pet boom to the lack of emotional friction promised by human–pet relationships because any obscured frictions lead to the exact contradictions to which she was drawing attention. Dissenting voices were at great pains to psychoanalyze her "abnormality" (see Nakamura 2010, 10). Many rebuttals—notably, one by Sakonji—saw a contradiction in Bandō's logic, which spoke of kittens as existing within the sphere of a cat's "life" even as she described her conscious deprivation of it. In pointing out as much, Sakonji ignored the fact that humans are constantly being killed to prove any number of social, political, or legislative points. It was a crest that went unaddressed in the first wave of criticism when Bandō was merely turning those questions back on the rest of us. Haters looked away, preferring to anoint her victims in martyrdom.

More than overlooked, Bandō's argument was fiercely and willfully ignored. Nakamura has no compunctions echoing Bandō in her assessment of hypocrisy. The problem, as he sees it, "is with modern Japanese society on the whole, not just between people and pets: the significance of life common to all living things has become sullied" (14). One could expand his argument to say that the more "liberal" the society, the more animal life becomes expendable. As Inokuma Hisashi (2001, 164) notes: "In liberal societies, industry continues to produce as long as there is demand. The consumers come first." Pets are products of a self-indulgent enterprise "having no more value than any other commodity in a consumer society." The idea of a product possessing "life" is heretical. Bandō has consciously performed what many do unconsciously on a daily basis. Could it be that her enemies revile her because they revile themselves?

Amid this defensive storm was a voice of reason from Kobayashi. Noting that "in Japan upward of 400,000 dogs and cats abandoned by irresponsible owners are euthanized at health care centers every year," he attributed the sudden spike in abandoned animals to the pet boom itself as people were buying pets without sufficiently considering the responsibilities involved. For him, so-called animal welfare centers were "not a far cry from Auschwitz" (Nakamura 2010, 15–16). The gas chambers used for daily euthanizing are known as "dream boxes" (doriimu bokkusu), a euphemism that betrays an inability to cope with their purpose. After a week, unclaimed dogs and cats are herded into these chambers and killed with a carbon dioxide cocktail to "become repositories for the selfishness of owners' negligence" (15).

Kobayashi's 2006 book, also called Dream Boxes, was released just two months before Bandō's ill-fated article yet was favorably received for relegating the problematic act of killing to a salary-sanctioned public service. Though dream box killings are routine, "the staff must forcibly herd dogs and cats, who defecate out of sheer terror as they desperately resist, and watch as they scream when the gas is turned on, eyes rolling back as they drop to the floor, foaming at the mouth" (16). While conducting interviews at welfare centers across Japan, Kobayashi discovered that dream box operators believe owners should take responsibility by killing their pets themselves, noting that for every individual who cherishes a pet as a family member are many who toss pets aside like so much waste once they have outlived their usefulness or interest. Every time Kobayashi observed this horror firsthand, he thought, "I am being shown a part of the true state of Japan and its people" (17). Kobayashi followed this thread to its source by interviewing Bandō. In that interview, she highlights the stress taken on by welfare center workers, who must deal with their roles as hatchet persons for a cowardly public.

Bandō was unsatisfied with the pet-boom narrative. In an open rebuttal, published in the September 16, 2006, issue of *Shūkan Gendai*, she coined the term "sterilization of love" (*ai no funin*) to describe what she saw as a pervasive modern sickness. It allows us to pour love into pets as substitutes for a real love we fear giving to each other and ourselves. Instead, love has been replaced by adoration for pets, themselves sterilized in return for their affections, as if to keep those affections centered on us. The act of sterilizing pets is a form of denial that lies naked once someone like Bandō breaks the fourth wall surrounding it. People can only react with hatred because they take her killing of kittens personally. Bandō ends her rebuttal: "I suffer from a sickness one might call the sterilization of love, and all this commotion over 'Killing Kittens' has come from those similarly afflicted. They are the ones attacking me as crazy, even as I search for a way out. What I've come to realize after going through this turmoil is that society is patently sick. Isn't it about time we stopped this abnormal attack against kitten killing, peer into the abyss of Japanese society in which this phenomenon occurs, and hash it out?" (cited in Nakamura 2010, 21–22). Rather than blame pet-boom psychology or the "self-centered ideologies of animal welfare groups," Bandō made a case for a "far-reaching pathology, a discord of human relations in the rotted corridors of modern Japanese hearts" (22).

In premodern Japan, unwanted dogs and cats were unceremoniously tied up in bags and tossed into rivers. No one seemed to have a problem with it then, and this practice continues in rural areas. Bandō attributes the change in attitude to the rise of capitalism, which loves animals only out of a need for balance. Protecting animals prevents them from being used up as marketable resources, as in the preservation efforts of whales and pandas, which spell lucrative business for water parks and zoos worldwide. But we live in a society that conceals its discomforts and would much rather replace one problem with another.

The circularity of this debate goes back to Bandō's rebuttal, in which she highlights the disproportionate number of lives taken by human beings every year (through abortions, factory farming, etc.). The target of her critique is an arbitrary hierarchy of animal worth, which holds that animals raised as pets are worth more than those raised for food.

Japan's pathological obsession, says Bandō, has resulted in a sterilization of our love for one another. The "love" with which we have replaced
the genuine article consists of lavishing affection on animals in place
of humans while modifying those animals through forced sterilization.
This sickness is a direct symptom of our fear of love's impotence. We
repress that fear until it breaks through as animal abuse. Consequently,
"the moment we hear the words 'Killing Kittens,' we recoil from that
shock as if we were the ones being killed, and we erupt with hatred
toward the one doing the killing" (21). If anything is truly abnormal, in
Bandō's mind, it is the attack being sustained against her.

The Sin of Becoming

Upon seeing footage of pets left homeless by the 2011 Tōhoku earthquake and tsunami, the filmmaker Inudō Isshin (2013) remarked, "The
eye of the camera looms over them, capturing something of the human
heart in all those animals displaced by the earthquake. There's a spark
of life in their eyes. They stare at the camera as if to say, 'Are you just
going to stand there and watch us die?'" It is not unusual to read human
suffering into animals displaced by catastrophe. The impact of natural
disasters blurs the lines between communities because the power of cli-
mate reminds us we are subordinate to greater forces just as animals
may be to theirs. We reach out in humility to animals for solace, desiring
completion of a circuit we take for granted.

Like the footage that sparked Inudō's comment, writing is a "technovisual" process in which the exigencies of becoming succumb to categorical breakdown. As an emblematic medium by which one might
best understand personal connections to (and disconnections from)
animals, writing provides an intermediary space in which visions of animals may be scrutinized. Animality comes to be fixed even as humanity
encompasses it in a sphere of continual change. In a sense, animality is
immortal. It precedes us and will outlive us, a "wild" core of biological
existence from which humans have become separated in postlapsarian
fantasies of progress. When the animal dies or is close to dying, it rends
the fabric of social order. Literature survives as a persistent apparatus
by which an overwhelming plenitude of errors coheres as words and
sentences, allowing readers the benefit of private scrutiny.

According to pattrice jones (2007, 161), self-imposed dissociations
from nature and other animals are traumas in and of themselves. These
dissociations are necessary initiations into human individuation. As a

process of becoming activated by literary production, trauma challenges long-held anthropomorphisms, which assume that "people understand things by *attributing* characteristics *to* them" rather than "by *perceiving* characteristics *in* them" (Milton 2005, 255–56, original emphases). Kay Milton offers the term "egomorphism" to better describe the process by which "ego" or "self" becomes "the primary point of reference for understanding both human and non-human things" (255). Writing produced and consumed by human beings reinforces the egomorphic angle.

The separation of humans from animals consistently reinscribes itself. One repeats the story of the lost or abused pet because it affords a retelling of that trauma. The story becomes part of the collective memory—or forgetting, as the case may be—of schisms between species and environments, of which one seeks recovery through productive error. Stories about pets inform environmental understandings because one holds on to those relationships as proof of actual contact. In treating contact as substitution, one furthers themselves from animals and treats this separation as a trauma. The assertion of trauma itself becomes a trauma to replace the trauma being ignored.

Vicki Hearne (1994), a philosopher and animal trainer who sought reciprocity in her relationship with animals, provides an illustration by way of Fyodor Dostoyevsky, whose humanistic Ivan Karamazov cannot tolerate a world in which even a single person suffers. "This is a distinctively human option," Hearne notes, "not a position any animal in my ken has it in his or her power to take." She elaborates: "But there are aspects of human ethics—nowadays *largely confused with morality*—that overlap matters that can occupy animals, or some animals. Animals are capable of conscientiousness, of a fastidiousness about what matters to them and their fellows, including their human fellows, that in some cases puts us to shame, or at least often puts me to shame, but as far as I know there are no brooding Ivan Karamazovs among the nonhuman animals, who may therefore have a greater gift for accepting happiness than we do" (xv, my emphasis). Ivan's concern surmounts the borders of immediate corporeality and is defined by sympathy as an extension of the self so that denial of abuse becomes a way of life. His ethics are self-serving. While animals would seem to have a "natural" gift for accepting happiness, human beings thwart it with philosophical parries. Through the invention of moral fictions, human beings see themselves as highly evolved creatures and, through their works, treat animals as themselves. Error enters through a stubborn belief that our duty as intelligent agents is to espouse morality in the face of ignorant regimes of the natural. Ethical concern for animals, as Hearne defines it, does not embrace animals but overlaps with them. The difference is that an animal does not share this concern for the well-being of others as a moral construct. Instead of crying for a broken world, an animal frolics through a landscape watered by tears.

When Jean Baudrillard (2001, 83) writes, "Words do not respect the limits of meaning; they continually mingle with parallel significations," he means to say that the constituted self and the other live separately, achieving eternal sameness only in death. Literature, as a mediation of perception, allows one to "jump tracks" and, through animals' alterity, invites awareness of multiple existences. Baudrillard implicitly defines literature as a simulation that sets arbitrary, albeit pervasive, binaries of mediation against firsthand experience. Bandō blames not only perception but also attribution for degrading the human–pet relationship. It is one thing to perceive a pet as a family member, quite another to attribute humanity to a pet that possesses nothing of the sort.

If it seems difficult to read trauma into this relationship, Bandō would say it is because we have allowed ourselves to become sick with the sterilization of love from which she herself suffers. Even as trauma may seem to reduce the number of ethical factors at play in prose, it opens them to productive errors. The "unity of events" presented by animal literature enables disruptions of language, space, and time across a spectrum. Trauma is not an external threat but an internal quality of trans-species relations by which empathy can be either completely ignored or fortified to the point of hyperbole. "Only in the literary text," says Akira Mizuta Lippit (2000, 134), "does the animal remain in the body as a foreign element without, at the same time, corrupting that body irreversibly. Literature can be seen [as] a vaccine against itself and the animality it harbors." The act of telling (and retelling) ensures that only the lessons we feel comfortable with will be highlighted.

If literature is a collective enterprise, then it must harbor collective traumas. In this sense, I nod to Carl Cassegård (2014, 14), who by "collective" means "not simply a trauma that is shared among a number of people" but "damage sustained by discursive systems that hold collectives together." As a discursive system, literature sustains the damage of humans' separation from environments at large by rubbing salt into that disruption through the over-intensification of trans-species bonds. Following Cassegård further, we must be careful not to give literature too much credit for its discursive power, distinguishing as he does "in not regarding trauma as an identity position formulated *in* discourse" but as "something that happens *to* discourse, a damage that renders certain things hard to verbalize and express" (16). Rather than assert a humanized "us" in relation to an animalized "them," as has Bandō, in the next section, I break down those categories and the interactions between them.

Trauma crosshatches a moment in which mind, body, and circumstance become indistinguishable, when divides between realms of experience are foreshortened beyond a subject's control. In the case of Bandō's killings, the animals' explicit absence—their erasure, if you will, from the scripture of accountability—makes their imperatives that much more present in the minds of those who yearn for resurrection. It is unlikely that Bandō's killings are to be interpreted as a new beginning—unlikelier still that they will be taken as a paradigm shift.

Saying an animal triggers a traumatic response in human beings is not the same as saying an animal is inherently traumatic. Owning a pet is, under humane circumstances, a situation that lives by the animal's patterns and preferences (taking the dog out for a walk, for instance). Anyone who does not abide by the animal's patterns is said to be abusive or neglectful and subject to the law. But to do this on a more massive scale, as a society, is no longer criminal because its influence is too widespread to enable a terror of individual blame. In this sense, Bandō has scapegoated herself so that others might come forward in solidarity.

Whether pet owners see themselves through the Bandō lens is irrelevant because neither mindset challenges the servitude of the animal in a domestic setting. But is it really that animals are subordinated to human beings by way of direct action? Or is it that we are subordinating ourselves to misinterpretations of pastoral power through egomorphic projection? It is not entirely unwarranted to see animals as victims of literary violence by which their bodies become torn and remade, for such is the nature of remembrance. A promise between what is fragmented and remembered has been broken and, through literature, is restored. Readers mourn the loss of Bandō's kittens not because they have been killed but because the readers themselves are still alive.

Debating Bandō

Of the three protracted debates included in *On "Killing Kittens,"* the most productive is that between Bandō and Higashi, who speaks of people burning Bandō's books in the grossest political terms. "The public enjoys fascism," says Higashi, who also quotes Ikeda Hiroshi, a historian of German fascism: "Modern Japanese people hunger for blood" (cited in Bandō 2009, 85). For this reason, argues Higashi, the public mistook Bandō's admission to mean that she *wanted* to kill those kittens out of sadistic enjoyment and that any such self-projections were indicative of her detractors' hunger for blood. They took her apparent sadism as a sign she wanted to kill *them* in kind. They retaliated by demanding her death as recompense.

Bandō is quick to assert that her killings were the result not of calculated desire but of frantic desperation. Her confession was an act of atonement. She draws an equal sign between sterilizing cats and killing their offspring. While pet ownership and breeding might seem like comfort zones in which animals safely live out their lives, forced sterilization equates them to slaves. Letting them die without aid is no different than euthanizing them. In this way, Bandō notes, people have lost touch with the true meaning of abundance. They live in a society of *regulated* abundance, which serves as a distraction from death. Bandō and Higashi agree that separations of good and evil are not so clear today and that more and more people are thinking less and less about death and dying. When Bandō encounters an online comment that says, "I feel like I want to throw up," she knows readers see a kitten's death as their own. Such responses associate cute kittens with some concept of a "good life" (99), while holding no remorse for the invasive mosquitos or centipedes she squashes at home.

Bandō and Higashi touch on the topic of peace activism, especially as it relates to post-Hiroshima politics, and doubt any utopian idealism in which peace necessarily equals good and war evil (104). There is a sea change to be interpolated: that maintenance of peace is predicated on violence. Modern urban environments like Hiroshima enjoy the privileges born of violent pasts, which, despite haunting the present with reminders of unthinkable atrocity, validate widespread commitments to peace. But had no such violence ever occurred, who is to say whether peace would be such a rallying hub? Bandō is making a similar, if implicit, argument: Our love for animals is but a drop in the tide of their longstanding mistreatment. Until we recognize that, we are doomed to perpetuate violence. The entire food industry, which in developed nations promises peace (a well-fed people are a complacent people), would not exist without the violence of slaughter. And in rural environments, where people live off local land and wildlife, killing is a part of daily life. Bandō's point is simple: In the animal rights game, it is all or nothing.

Sympathies for animals, insofar as they are expressed only in reaction to a tragedy, are emblematic of a privileged, middle-class sentimentality toward animals. Even though such postcolonial outrage hinges on the acceptance of a natural imaginary—or is it an imaginary nature?—it is limited to the internet channels taking Bandō to task. It is indicative of a prepolitical mode of thought, whereby the public latches on to a cause without engaging it to the point of organized action. For this reason, Bandō was put off by readers who sought to apply Japanese laws to events that occurred in Tahiti. Though her detractors were perfectly willing to extend the laws of their home nation to one of their own gone bad, they seemed content ignoring the systematic animal killings supported by that same legal system on their home turf. Neoliberal sympathies thrive on the selective subjugation of egomorphic idealism.

Bandō's admission showed readers a slice of human behavior they never wished to see: that we speak of pets as endearing creatures from a self-centered worldview. People reacted vociferously to Bandō's killings because cats are mirrors of this self-love that humans enjoy. She was calculated in choosing the verb "to kill" (*korosu*) over "to discard" (*suteru*) to describe her actions because she saw no difference between the two. Her readers took this to mean that killing was the be-all and end-all of who she was and that anything in between constituted mindless filler. They saw no reflection because her mirror was fully splattered with their guilty conscience.

Dueling Bandōs

Bandō's outing of selective animal interests teases out a weakness in the animal rights debate: No one can agree on what constitutes animals in relation to (if at all different from) human beings. If animal rights are indeed empty and constructed through feigned concern for the lives of others, the Bandō controversy drives the debate into new territory in a Japanese literary vehicle.

Pets represent not nature but an "intense urbanization of the human zone" (Csicsery-Ronay 2014) and are prone to multiple meanings. Gilles Deleuze and Félix Guattari (1987, 245) unpack the nature of multiplicity, which for them "is defined not by the elements that compose it in extension, not by the characteristics that compose it in comprehension, but by the lines and dimensions it encompasses in 'intension.'" The idea of an animal as a multiplicity begins and ends with that animal, an involution on a larger scale. The moment one recognizes a pet as a companion, questions arise that owners are unprepared to answer. Helena Pedersen (2011, 73) poses one of them: "At what point does 'companion species' slip into 'companion speciesism'?" The Bandō controversy suggests that Japanese pet-boom culture would be nothing without companion speciesism.

If pet keeping is a pathological behavior, it is symptomatic of how postmodern people think about the nature of their (disbelief in) souls by reducing interspecies contact to an illusion of mind over matter. Like euthanasia, the human–animal relationship is a curious ratio of empathy and cruelty and explodes at death into something personal, a fear beyond reproach. Harlan Miller (2009, 63) prettily words the conundrum: "[I]f it were true that humans have immortal souls and nonhumans lack them, that would not provide any reason to give priority to human interests. It would, rather, support assigning priority to the interests of nonhumans." In this statement, one faces the arrogance of those who mistake awareness for the primacy of being. One must fear the possibility of things without souls, lest humans lack them.

Witnessing the death of a pet activates an anxiety over soullessness. At that moment, the animal becomes human, and vice versa, to the point where "we can no longer hold up the edifice of difference. We all become liminal creatures" (Pierce 2012, 222). To this philosophical line of flight, the authors surveyed herein add another, for witnessing the *life* of a pet also activates this fear, of which Bandō's writing is a vivid reminder. In taking responsibility for death, she bids readers to take responsibility for life.

To validate a universal category of "the animal," we must continue to hold nature accountable for failures in ourselves. Insistence on animals as social outsiders or outcasts should be taken not as a need to rescue them but as a point of continuity to be meticulously shaped like clay on a potter's wheel. All of this piles up like psychological currency that, in the words of Baudrillard (2001, 3), "cannot be exchanged for either truth or for reality." This means the written word, as a function of a literary mindset, is not the only criterion by which reality may be measured. Its affective grammar, too, has a direct bearing on nature. In other words, the possible ways we might define experience are mutually dependent on how those ways regard or define us. We see animals as obstacles because they regard us in species-specific ways we codify through sciences and theories of form and being.

Another Sacred Secret

In a memorial piece posted online in 2014, the famed mystery novelist Higashino Keigo recalls a meeting with his friend, Bandō. It has been some time since their last, and Higashino relishes the opportunity to catch up with her at a bar upon her final return to Japan. Like many readers, Higashino was naturally taken aback by "Killing Kittens." He steers the conversation in that direction. Bandō admits to being pleased by the backlash for proving her point. Higashino agrees with the philosophy behind her actions but insists her method for putting that philosophy into effect crossed a line. Bandō sets him straight: "It's not like that at all. People see the word 'cliff' and imagine some towering precipice when it was really no more than a two-meter drop into soft brush; the fall wouldn't have killed them. In actuality, I only threw the kittens into a grassy area out back." Bandō had used the word "killing" because she saw no difference between her actions and separating kittens from their mother. She never expected readers to take her admission so literally.

Higashino wants Bandō to be remembered as a "writer of great novels" (*subarashii shōsetsu o kaku hito*), but his efforts have gone undetected. Bandō's message retains validity even as most of its recipients would rather hold on to some illusion of her villainy than acknowledge any possibility of their own. "Killing Kittens" was not an act of proselytization, despite being taken as such. It was a social contract left unsigned. In getting her point across, Bandō relied too heavily on the power of language in the hopes that others might reassess their role in its harm. By then, however, the damage had been done. Bandō's kittens had already tumbled fatally from the towering cliffs of readers' minds.

CHAPTER 2

A Canine Triptych

This chapter is divided into three sections covering various genres. Genre is especially important in film, where it functions in Part 1 as a process rather than a fixed set of criteria. As our relationships with animals shift over time, so do the ways in which those relationships are portrayed on screen. Dramatized animals are psychological beacons of moral messages. The dog constitutes an all-inclusive package of sensitivity, unconditional acceptance, and softening of species lines. As conveyed in Part 1, the Japanese film *10 Promises to My Dog* (*Inu to watashi no jū no yakusoku*, hereafter, *Promises*; 2008, directed by Katsuhide Motoki) is a sonata of animal appropriation. Its leitmotif of guilt is rooted in birth, kinship, and parenthood. In it lies a wealth of good intentions and gross fabrications alike, allowing us to see the ways in which canine cinema can be progressive yet questionable in its commitment to animal well-being. This genre may just be the most productive error of them all.

Parts 2 and 3 concern themselves with biographies and autobiographies about disability. Whether in the guide-dog literature of the late twentieth and early twenty-first centuries or in the inspirational story of a dog without limbs, the examples provided here share an affinity for bodies at odds with ableist norms. Because we are ready and willing to have conversations about impairment when their catalyst is a likeable animal while, in the same breath, denying complicity in the abuse and discrimination of disabled people, some fantasy of unblemished humanity reigns supreme. Until we do something to challenge this notion, we remain beholden to ourselves and to the individual animals on whom we depend.

Part 1: A Lick and a Promise

> "Scale, space, stories are all anthropomorphic."
> —Laura Mulvey (1988, 60)

Laura Mulvey, in her 1975 essay "Visual Pleasure and Narrative Cinema," effectively turned the gaze of cinema back on itself. At the time, Mulvey was speaking to the contrivance of mise-en-scène, of its human motivations and human targets, and of the conventions by which its voyeuristic pleasures were built on, around, and through women's bodies. Cinema's technicality presented them as incomplete, fetishized, and ready for surrender. Though focused on women, Mulvey's theoretical cartography can be mapped onto animals as parallel targets of psychological and physical abuse. This is not to suggest that women are like animals or vice versa—only that the grammar of moving pictures renders them both invisible.

Cinema has always had a close relationship with animals. The coincidence of its technological occurrence with the rise of Darwinism meant that animals, as objects of study, were easily adapted to visual media for scientific and archival value. The theory of natural selection had effectively secularized the universe, painting human beings as "simply one species among many" (Creed 2009, xiv). Once separate, animals and humans shared the same progeny, the same building blocks of life, and the same motivations for survival. Charles Darwin's takeaway was that humans may not be the center of life.

Darwin was by no means immune to values. As became clearer in his later work, he had been following a decidedly human moral compass all along, relegating what he saw as unidirectional animal instincts to the realm of savagery. (Let us not forget the full title of his 1859 magnum opus: *On the Origin of Species by Means of Natural Selection, or the Preservation of Favoured Races in the Struggle for Life*.) Darwin's curiosity spread comfortably and vividly into the "human-beast cycles" of early cinema (xiii). Archetypal examples of these include *King Kong* and *Tarzan of the Apes*, both of which expanded the possibilities of human–animal relations in the collective conscience by scrutinizing two sides of the same evolutionary coin: the extent to which an animal could be accepted on broader social terms and the extent to which a human being could "pass" for an animal.

Ideally, the medium of film should record things as they are, indifferent to whatever is projected. Yet as technologies developed (and scholarship with them), film, like science, became a realm of contradiction. Suddenly, we were no longer watching but gazing, no longer archiving but favoring, and no longer filming but shooting. The cutting room became a kill floor and the framing of bodies an act of violence. Animal bodies were worked into the medium of film as its message, only later emerging as fully drawn characters whose actions became central to plot development and empathic audience response. Yet animals had long enlivened the moving image with subjective concerns by displacing humans as purveyors of the modern.

Animals are more than canvasses. As living, thinking beings, they cannot be relegated to the role of an object or prop, despite their dramatic function, any more than human actors. Likewise, their roles are multifarious. On the one hand, cinematic animals are products of technologies (e.g., training tools and regimens) that are "far more dependent on the actual physical existence of real animals," who serve as "active coproducers in shaping human discussions about them" (Skabelund 2011, 16). As catalysts for action, animals exist for viewer titillation. Recognizing them as actors validates their involvement in the processes undermining or exploiting that involvement.

Animals in film have human *and* nonhuman qualities. The former invariably reign supreme, which may explain why films about humans turning into animals are far more common than the reverse. Only when animals have been activated by the human do they become suitable for philosophical and ethical disclosure. It is tempting, therefore, to read animals with discursive consistency across media. This may not be the wisest approach, as differences abound. While it is beyond the scope of this chapter, I would be remiss not to point the reader to Thomas LaMarre (2008), who has keenly noted the prevalence of animals in animation, "which seems bent on expressing animal invulnerability, where cinema tends to linger on animal fragility." In other words, LaMarre continues, "cinema humanizes animals, while animation tends to animalize humans" (82).

The medium of film has fundamentally challenged the human-animal divide. Having "created a different order of the animal, one whose agency (desires, dreams) challenges the bases on which the differences between human and animal have historically and philosophically been founded" (Creed 2009, 178), film enriches our understanding of animal minds and strengthens our relationship with animals in real life. By including animals as bona fide characters, cinema is supposed to have given us valuable insight into nonhuman thinking. In practice, this has not been the case.

The more we make films about animals, the more human they become. Cinematic animals are "ontological hybrids"—they embody multiple subject positions across species lines (Jeong 2011, 179–80). Over time, montage has painstakingly constructed and reproduced this illusion of "human animals," as many animals that would otherwise have no connection to or interest in us in the wild are defined in filmic space through their relationships with humans. Therefore, the absence of humans tends to come across as an expression of pure animality. In the movies, this expression becomes documentarian. Such realism stems from the whims of filmed subjects, whose indeterminate actions are allowed free reign to look as "natural" as possible without intervention, even in the face of mortal danger. And yet, the brilliance of film is that it so snugly fits illusions into our perceptions. Nature documentaries often feature killings despite the fact that these are relatively infrequent events, especially among larger mammals, and may be the results of hours of waiting and countless botched attempts.

Just as Christine Gledhill (1999, 267) once asked, "Can women speak, and can images of women speak for women?" it behooves us to pose the same question in reference to animals. While none but the most ignorant of us would ever have the audacity to claim that women are inherently voiceless, a disproportionate percentage of us could get away with claiming so for animals. Gledhill, however, takes issue with the very premise of the question itself. "The ultimate problem," she asserts, "lies in the attempt to make language and the signifying process so exclusively central to the production of social formation" (271). By treating language as the primary building block of any social nexus, animals are excluded from the possibility of sharing our spotlight. They can only be recipients of our care: ever the pet, the child, the locus for entertainment.

While animals are, as fictional creations, puppets of the cinematic imagination, and nothing if not projections of viewers' disturbances, animal actors bring unpredictable and uncontrollable aspects to any film production in which they are involved. This distinction between objectification and being is most fuzzily blurred in dogs, who are "neither nature, nor culture, not both/and, not neither/nor, but something else" (Haraway 2011, 158). As such, dogs cannot always, if ever, be restricted to one of these categories.

Animal cinema is conventionally lumped under the rubric of the "family film." This cooption serves viewers by welcoming animals as equals and by allowing us to see them as morally minded creatures committed to the preservation of life. This twofold process has a dark side. In addressing animals on human terms, such films send a contradictory message: that in order for animals to be moral beings, they must first be "elevated" to a human level by giving themselves up for our sake. While classics abound in Hollywood—*Lassie*, *Rin Tin Tin*, and *Old Yeller* not least among them—self-sacrifice is central to all manner of canine prototypes, for it necessarily disguises animal worth with an attractive veneer of individuality. This, too, is a sham, for what adjectives might we use to describe Lassie that we might not also use to describe any other hero? Loyalty is not a marker of personality but a right for and of which the animal body is a living vessel. Lassie, by practically any other name, breed, or species, would accomplish and evoke no less.

Why the attraction? Why do we have an apparent willingness to watch a dog perish, if only to protect her master? Why might we witness a dog's act of bravery and think to ourselves, "If only *my* dog were like that," or, "If only *we* were like that"? This is why the most enduring canine narratives, like the aforementioned, tend to take place in nostalgic rural canvases across which to paint moral pictures, far removed from the city, where the pace of life leaves neither people nor animals with much space or time to ponder the deeper questions of modern ennui. Whether computer-generated or trained, the canine of twenty-first-century cinema has even less of a personality than it did before, despite the fact that now, more than ever, dogs talk, emote, sing, dance, solve crimes (and commit them), save the world, cry, complain about cats to no end, communicate and work with other species, love, fight, dream, meditate, eat, chase, and (on occasion) even bark. In portraying dogs in such a way, the film industry's attempt to impart agency to these canines has emptied them of it.

For the sake of argument, assume cinematic animals *do* have independent minds. In that case, three false premises must be accepted: 1) animals are worthy creatures insofar as they can be understood unambiguously on *our* terms; 2) animals hide their true selves from us, and we can only access their secrets through violence and exploitation; and 3) without us, animals would live in chaos. While there are aspects of consciousness we may never fully understand in any animal, much less ourselves, such assumptions provide no moral grounds on which to build a philosophy of domination. By the same token, the prevalence of cinematic animals stems from a genuine desire to instill a belief in, and respect for, their individuality. All the more unfortunate, then, that canine cinema is having the opposite effect. There is no reason to suspect any malicious intent to disconnect us from animal consciousness. That being said, there is something highly problematic about the cinematic dog, whose choices, while made under the guise of self-selection, have only us in view. The dog's well-being is rarely primary, and therein lies its value as a productive error.

Dogs are not metaphors. Treating them as such "allows the symbolic significance of their existence to overshadow their tangible interactions with people" (Skabelund 2011, 17). Still, what dogs do for us in these capacities is undeniable. Not only do they provide service through the jobs by which we employ them, but as "figures," they give back all that we invest in them with interest. The intensity of their involvement in human lifeways is unique among companion species and allows for an especially insightful (and exploitable) ethical relationship. As Donna Haraway (2011, 158) puts it, "We have necessarily to be in an ethical relationship with dogs, because they are vulnerable to human cruelty in very particular ways, or to carelessness, or stupidity." Because dogs would not be here without us, they appear more than any other animal in film. Consequently, viewers may be lured into thinking *no* animal would survive without us.

Perceived differences between humans and animals are relative. The same mindset that roots human malice in the bestial also frames animals' affirmational qualities as moral imperatives. Dogs ride the wave of posthumanism insofar as they are imprinted by the interference of difference. Yet dogs are more than just "in-betweeners," for they must be "other" before they can be anything else. Canine cinema simultaneously amplifies and hushes animality to achieve a specific emotive effect.

Dogs are not one half of a dichotomy but the dichotomy of one half. They exist in opposition to us while embodying vibrant contradictions of agency and passivity; they represent but are not themselves representations. Because their existence implies an "obligatory relationship with human beings" (158), whatever dogs may do is absorbed by the dominant trope of loyalty, in which the only variations are of degree and not of kind. Dogs are not surrogate children. "When you live with a dog," Haraway reminds us, "you live with *another adult* who is not your species" (159). As living, breathing adults, dogs are capable of self-cultivation and awareness, which is why cinematic dogs tend *not* to be infantilized. Rather than surrogate children, they are more often portrayed as surrogate parents or caretakers. The film *Promises* realizes the possibility of parentage from an animal's perspective like no other piece of Japanese canine cinema.

A "Promising" History

Japanese canine cinema would be nothing without Hachikō (1923–35), the loyal dog who famously waited for his dead master at a Tokyo railway station for nearly a decade during Japan's interwar period (1918–39). Hachikō epitomizes what Aaron Skabelund (2011) calls "canine imperialism," under which the presence of dogs reinforced colonial attitudes. With canine imperialism came an influx of breeds, with breeds the possibility of political traction, and with both an opportunity for elites to exploit their dogs as signifiers of power between and during the wars. In line with this assessment, LaMarre (2008, 92) goes so far as to say that Japan's particular version of speciesism was "the wartime attempt to get out of racism through animal cooperation."

Breed, like race, is a cultural phenomenon linked to the rise of the nation-state. The double leash of language and culture kept canines close at hand even as it pushed them away. Loyalty, civilization, and race hinged on an allegiance to the efficacy of domestication, which sought to quell savagery and open the future to the wonders of civil expansion. Canine imperialism is a hybrid product of human and animal intentionality insofar as dogs took it upon themselves to gain an advantage over their canid ancestors by siding with humans: a provocative twist on the animal-as-moral-patient trope that views dogs as unwitting pawns in human colonial games while acknowledging their behavioral contributions—conditioned as they were—to regimes of civil morality.

Hachikō spurred public interest in unified ethnic nationalism. Yet, despite being a member of a "native" species, his blood was far from pure. There is nothing "pure" about breeding in the first place, relying as it does on habitual isolation, by which manipulative actors shape the flow of genes into desired pools and patterns. Like the constructions of race in which colonialism was steeped, Japan's bid for purity came at a critical juncture of global changes. Hachikō was tuned to be a crucial instrument for the revitalization of national dogs, belying concerted efforts between the Ministry of Education and Japan's growing number of dog enthusiasts to even the scales not only of human progress but also of animal mind—so long as it was *Japanese* animal mind that stood to benefit.

Hachikō's sacrifice was the nation's sacrifice. To think that this kind-hearted animal, "a product of culture as much as of nature" (Skabelund 2011, 107), could have been subjected to such corruption is a reminder of the illocutionary power of promulgation in delicate times. His dedication carried weight because he was an animal one could relate to and in whom one could visualize a hopeful future when ethnic purity was pinned under foreign microscopes.

When director Kōyama Seijirō made *Hachikō's Tale* (*Hachikō monogatari*, 1987), he was committing a Derridean "fabulization," in which a subject of broad interest "remains an anthropomorphic taming, a moralizing subjection, a domestication. Always a discourse *of* man, on man, indeed on the animality of man, but for and in man" (Derrida 2008, 37). As it happens, the feature film was released at a time when Japan's economic bubble was nearing its bursting point. Note, too, the contrast in reception when the film was revived through the star power of Richard Gere and Joan Allen in the 2009 remake, *Hachi: A Dog's Tale* (directed by Lasse Hallström). That American producers saw fit to wait twenty-two years speaks to the latent need for its message outside of Japan. That the film was never shown in American theaters speaks further to its lack of traction in Hollywood.

Hachikō's moral messages were reworked in the film *A Tale of Mari and Three Puppies* (*Mari to koinu no monogatari*; 2007, directed by Inomata Ryūichi), which dramatizes the true story of three Shiba Inu born just before the 2004 Niigata earthquake and their courageous mother who saved them and her human family. These puppies, like Hachikō, were said to embody the core values of their breed, and their nation by extension, in a time of crisis: spiritedness (*kan'i*), good-naturedness (*ryosei*), and innocence (*soboku*).

In 2004, the canine cinematic landscape was redrawn once again with the release of *Quill* (*Kuiiru*; directed by Sai Yōichi), yet another true story, this time of a Labrador retriever whose brief life touched many before the film was made. As the most successful dog biography since *Hachikō's Tale*, it was instrumental in sparking a canine renaissance in Japan's film and literary industries. Its themes were further developed in 2010's *Partners* (*Paatonaazu*; directed by Shimomura Masaru), in which another Labrador retriever comes into his own as a guide dog through the joys and tribulations of those who care for him and are cared for by him. Yet it was in the 2006 miniseries *Dillon: Dog of Destiny* (*Diron:*

Unmei no inu) that the trope most relevant to the present discussion—motherhood—came into prominence. *Dillon* depicts a secluded housewife whose chance encounter with an abandoned golden retriever opens her to the possibilities of new friendship and betters her relationship with her husband and mother-in-law.

This brings us to *Promises*, which tells of a teenager whose mother, dying of terminal illness, gets a golden retriever puppy to replace her when she is gone. Before dying, she imparts ten promises from the dog's point of view in the hope her daughter will abide by them. The enormous success of *Promises* was built upon another enormous success: that of the promises themselves. If the opening page of the booklet that accompanies the special edition DVD of the film is to be believed, the titular "10 Promises" were supposed to have been posted online anonymously, often accompanied by a poem entitled "The Rainbow Bridge." Written from a dog's point of view to her master, they captured the hearts of online readers. They were so popular that they were "translated" by model Hasegawa Rie and published by Nihon Bungeisha in September of 2004 under the title of *The Dog's Ten Commandments* (*Inu no jukkai*). There is just one snag: The origin of these commandments is a fabrication.

In a day and age when true anonymity is hard to come by, I was suspicious of the mythical status the 10 Promises had achieved before the film monopolized them. Hours of research and email communication with authors and acquaintances clarified their mixed origin, summarized as follows.

In 1993, dog behaviorist and obedience trainer Stan Rawlinson wrote *The 10 Commandments from a Pet's Point of View*. Variously known as *The Dog's Ten Commandments* and *The Ten Commandments from a Dog's Point of View*, Rawlinson's widely circulated piece affected many dog owners and non-dog owners alike and was reposted on innumerable pet-related sites, online forums, Facebook walls, and other social media outlets where its message might have rung clear. Five years later, Stewart Metz, a medical doctor who quit his practice to found and run the Indonesian Parrot Project, would pen *A Parrot's Bill of Rights*. At the time, as Dr. Metz informed me via email, he knew nothing of Rawlinson's commandments, and indeed, the similarities are arbitrary at best. Striking, however, are the ways in which each immerses the reader in a nonhuman perspective. Both portray animals as desiring individuals whose personal happiness and understanding are necessary for peace of mind in a willful life.

Discrepancies arose in 1999 when Jane Hallander, an avian behavior specialist, posted what she called the *Ten Commandments of Parrot Ownership—From a Parrot's Point of View!* At first, Hallander passed these off as her own, despite having clearly copied and pasted them from Dr. Metz's lovingly crafted precepts. Only when Dr. Metz discovered this and contacted Hallander directly did she openly acknowledge their source. There is, however, one glaring difference between the two: Hallander added a few stipulations seemingly of her own, but which she actually lifted verbatim from Rawlinson's original commandments. Eventually, Hallander reduced the *Ten Commandments of Parrot Ownership* into a more manageable form, at which point they had become nothing more than an abbreviation of Rawlinson's.

At some point, while these commandments were making their rounds under Hallander's name, the word "parrot" reverted to "dog"—in deference, I can only surmise, to their origin. The newly speciated commandments appeared online in English alongside their Japanese translations. Credited as "author unknown," the *10 Commandments of Dog Ownership* caused a wave of emotional responses among internet readers. Many Japanese translations exist, but nearly always with the English in tow. The visual bilingualism of the commandments adds a ring of authority to their mythical impact, fueling the fallacy of their anonymity.

Not one month before the publication of *The Dog's Ten Commandments* saw the first, by Julian Publishing, under the same name, only this time with the added English subtitle, *The Ten Commandments, Dog Version, for Ownership*. While this would seem to indirectly acknowledge Hallander, the publishers still indicate the author as "unknown" and tout the book as the basis for the hit film. The persistence of this anonymity is disconcerting, for while the film credited a research team, the fact that even the most cursory Google search would have yielded *some* author (correct or not) undermines the integrity of this team and of any publishers banking on these evocative commandments. Whether or not this is a case of outright plagiarism is difficult to determine. Such productive errors are part and parcel of the film in question.

A Dog's Life Unfulfilled

Promises begins in total darkness. Anyone tempted to associate this void with the womb is rewarded, for the only diegetic clue given is the sound of whimpering puppies. Black space resolves into an image of their nursing mother cradled in hay, as if in some rural farmstead. Yet rather than

see this space as natal, we do better to see it as a tabula rasa, a vaguely sig-
nified palimpsest for the words that appear superimposed on the screen:

In the beginning, God created man,
but seeing him so feeble, He gave him the dog.

—Zoologist Alphonse Toussenel

A curious figure in whom to seek moral guidance for the ensuing tale,
Alphonse Toussenel (1803–85) espoused what he called *zoologie passion-
nelle,* or "passional zoology," a concept that regarded animals "from the
point of view of their moral, intellectual, and physical resemblance to
humans" (Kete 1994, 164). For Toussenel, animals were to humans as
humans were to God—not so much at the bottom of the moral hierarchy
as they were deferential to our quest for perfection.

What does it mean that a sentimental film begins with a quote from
someone once described as "a popular naturalist in whom is found a
paranoid mixture of anticapitalism, anti-industrialism, antiliberalism,
and anti-Semitism" (Kogan 2006, 290, n14)? A follower of the philosopher Charles Fourier (1772–1837), whose syndicalist approach to
social economy sought to abandon individualism altogether, Toussenel
fashioned a worldview that would later prove nourishing to Hitlerian
nationalism. Piggybacking on his Judeophobic tracts of 1845, Toussenel
produced three books on animals and birds. This trilogy was less about
animals and more about self-righteous commentary. As one indebted
to Fourier's theory of universal analogy, which posited that the binding glue of the cosmos was a "network of correspondences," Toussenel
envisioned a utopian state of harmony in which "humankind would at
least be reconciled with nature" and "creatures that embodied human
vices would disappear and new harmonious animals would be born"
(Crossley 2004, 463).

For every barrier between animals and humans he transcended, Toussenel put up another between humans and themselves. His zoology was
a means of venting social criticisms to fuel a personal xenophobia. Fourierism also preached a doctrine of cosmic love whereby the God-given
desires of humanity were said to enliven divine will. Such love could only
extend *to* animals rather than *from* them. Their essence, or "passion,"
could only be liberated when the exigencies of an unstable economy
and political order were restored to nature. Sewn into the very fabric of
nature, however, was humanity's dominion over animals. In this hierarchy, animals fell into three categories: 1) those that served man, 2) those
that merited preservation, and 3) those destined for extermination. The

first of these was further divided into "domestics" willingly offering themselves for human needs as food or clothing and "auxiliaries" to human power. The latter included dogs. In films like *Promises*, however, dogs are "emotional domestics," meaning they offer themselves willingly for human comfort and to ease anxiety.

Toussenel's animals were nothing more than signs, Nature nothing more than text. In this scheme, he fancied himself a translator of a *super-natural* message that, thanks to Fourierism, had apparently enlightened him to God's will. Toussenel "described the history of the animals as a literal translation of human history. In theory humans (and human history) had primacy and the animals had fixed meanings. In practice, however, Toussenel played with the possibilities of language and exploited ambiguities of meaning" (140). This view is significant and pervasive for depriving animals of language as a tool for manipulation. This view treats human experiences as innately primary, allows animals to be violated by human intentions, and gives human authors license to carry common tropes ("It's just fiction, after all!") into real life. The animal's individuality is not at stake, for the animal never loses it. It is simply unacknowledged. What *is* at stake is a life in which to exercise it.

Hence Toussenel's appearance in the opening frames, beyond which we now can proceed.

Promises introduces Saitō Akari, the fourteen-year-old daughter of a prominent surgeon and a middle schooler whose personality is about as vacuous as the film's inaugural fade from black. It is Akari's birthday, and her father, Yūichi, has been held up at work again, leaving her to celebrate with her mother, Fumiko. When Yūichi returns home at last, Akari is already in bed. During the conversation with her husband that follows, Fumiko mentions their daughter wants a dog, to which Yūichi quips, "To replace me?" In saying as much, he betrays the film's conceit.

Akari returns from school the next day. Seeing that no one is home, she goes into the back yard to take down the laundry, when she spots a golden retriever puppy in the bushes. As she proceeds to chase it, she is interrupted by the phone. On the other end is Yūichi, who explains her mother fainted and is in the hospital. As a medical doctor, Yūichi understands the gravity of his wife's terminal condition but assures Akari, as any loving parent might, her mother will be okay. As Akari takes on her mother's domestic duties, the puppy returns, much to the consternation of Yūichi, who flattens himself against a wall any time the harmless animal comes near. His mortal aversion to dogs is a redirect of his fear of being replaced.

Akari brings the puppy to the hospital, where Fumiko dubs her "Socks." Yet if Akari is going to keep Socks, Fumiko tells her, she must take the film's promises to heart. "Think like a dog," she bids. "I'll speak for her," at which point the promises are overlaid on the screen:

1. Listen patiently to what I have to say.
2. Trust me. I am always on your side.
3. Play with me a lot.
4. Don't forget that I have feelings, too.
5. Let's never fight. Someday I'll win.
6. If I don't obey you, I have a good reason.
7. You have school, and friends. But as for me, I only have you.
8. Stay my best friend, even when I'm old.
9. I'll live for about 10 years, so let's make every moment count.
10. Never forget our time together. Keep this in your mind. So when my time comes, please be by my side.

Throughout this exchange, the viewer begins to realize Fumiko surreptitiously bought the dog and had her "planted" so that Akari would find her. A clandestine way, to be sure, for her to exert parental authority in the face of dwindling mortality, just as Yūichi's insistence on Fumiko's recovery gives him reign over their daughter's emotional stability. Now armed with these commandments, Akari begins to awaken to her surroundings, as when, during a brief period of remission, Fumiko is walking along the beach with Akari, who remarks on being able to smell her mother's scent on the wind.

After Fumiko's death, Akari is watching TV with Socks when a news reporter interviews a veterinarian at the local Asahikawa Zoo. "Working with animals," he says, "is a strange experience. Animals are like people. Understanding how animals feel can often lead to an understanding of human emotions." It is then Akari realizes her true calling in life. To that end, a telling scene takes place just before her graduation when, after donning her mother's kimono, Socks dirties it by jumping on her as if trying to prevent Akari from coming into her own as an adult. What makes this all the more ironic is that, as Socks's most individual act, it is downplayed as abnormal behavior. Socks wants to be acknowledged, but Akari's goals take precedence. Suddenly, she becomes indifferent toward Socks, going so far as to scold Yūichi for spoiling her, and even complains to a friend, "Having a dog is so confining." Akari tells her father she has sacrificed so much for Socks and no longer has the will. She lands a job at the Asahikawa Zoo and leaves home. In Akari's absence, Yūichi takes a shine to the dog. "Because of you," he tells her, "Akari was never alone. She grew up happy." In saying as much, he effectively nullifies his role in her upbringing. He has come to grips with his inadequacy as a parent and with the pet who exposed it.

Only when Socks is on her deathbed does Akari race home to be at her faithful companion's side. Yūichi chooses this, of all moments, to give her a series of paintings Fumiko made while bedridden, each illustrating one of the ten promises. Akari reads through this relic of her late mother and wonders aloud whether she managed to follow through. Now aware that she has not followed through, Socks breathes her last, prompting Akari to expectorate a cathartic cry that she (presumably) never let out for mother. "If I stop talking to her, she'll die," Akari sobs, underlining Socks's role as a textual and linguistic trigger. Furthermore, while clearing out the doghouse, Akari and Yūichi find a stack of family photos that had previously gone missing. Among them is a letter from Fumiko addressed to Akari. It reads: *As long as Socks is alive, she can replace me. She'll look after you. But she won't live as long as you. So when her time comes, I will become the wind. Do you remember when you told me I was like the wind? The next time the wind blows, think of it as me.* And in the end, at Akari's wedding, Yūichi holds up pictures of Fumiko and Socks, ensuring no one will never forget that mother and dog were one and the same.

Chattling the Cage

Akari's career choice warrants a detour into the traumality of zoo-keeping in Japan. The famed Japanese educator and moral prescriber Fukuzawa Yukichi (1834–1901) was the first to coin the term *dōbutsuen* ("garden of animate things"). As the Japanese equivalent for "zoo," this neologism "owed a clear debt to corresponding nomenclature in the West, where the idea of animation and voluntary motion is closely tied to understandings of the animal" (Miller 2005, 297). Japanese readers first encountered the *dōbutsuen* in Fukuzawa's *Conditions in the West* (*Seiyō-jijō*), a three-volume work first published in 1866 that enjoyed great success for its frank Occidental observations. It also laid the groundwork for seeing nature as something not to be vied with but mastered. The cultural borrowing of this concept was significant, as by that time, "zoological gardens were a recognized gauge of national strength" (295). So did zoos activate the populace as a suitable testing ground for moral virtues in a fervently internationalizing Japan. Fukuzawa was one of many Japanese intellectuals whose travels away from the rising sun yielded a wealth of new ideas and practices. Their combined disciplinary calculus served Japan's emerging imperial project all too well. Confronted with apparent inadequacies, Japan struggled to assert itself globally through a voracious, if selective, adoption of Western trends. The appearance of Japanese zoos was one such response, emulating as it did the West's obsession with exhibitry and visual consumption.

American zoos at the time were invested in the promotion of the "native" landscape and its natural wonders. As intersections of the personal and political, these zoos had become breeding grounds for a very different kind of animal: patriotism. As newly fashioned "moral showcases," zoos provided "clearly recognizable venues for the display of national compassion towards the (seemingly) helpless, voiceless animals behind the bars" (276). Japan's most significant contribution was the Ueno Zoo. The nation's oldest, it was opened in Tokyo in 1882 and was the hub of an "animal management regime" (Knight 2011, 3). As such, it was "perhaps the grandest showcase for the public display of the Japanese nation-state's claims to cultural parity with the imperialist West in the late nineteenth century." In such delicate times, the humane maintenance of captive animals "arbitrated judgments about national civilization and racial or ethnic evolution in an age when such attributions could mean the difference between liberty and repression." As the "first zoological garden in Asia not constructed under a colonial regime," the Ueno Zoo was as much a primal cry for recognition as it was a lofty ornament of the same (Miller 2005, 291).

As the zoo grew in size and reputation, its animals shifted from being ambassadors of nature to outright cultural signifiers. Ueno's "highly ordered landscape" gave visitors insight into the nation's ability to mold time and space, transposing "the bewildering diversity of the natural world into a spectacular affirmation of Japanese humanity" (291). Ueno promoted "civilized curiosity," offset by the slew of merchandise associated with its animals, including many children's books, each an extension of the often-lengthy biographies on labels attached to every cage at the zoo. The animals were acculturated as subjects of a greater polity in which "nature" and "nation-state" became synonymous. Such "didactic spectacles" functioned as cultural barometers, whereby social capital was rationed out to those who subscribed to Japan's clout as a global power. The Ministry of Education went so far as to outlaw the use of English, now considered to be an "enemy language." As a result, zoo animals once designated by their English names were translated into cumbersome Japanese equivalents. Zoos grew far beyond the museums that Fukuzawa had imagined them to be, becoming more like amusement parks than educational institutions.

In times of strife, the Japanese archipelago did not hesitate to confirm the expendability of animals within its borders. An early instance took place in the First Sino-Japanese War (1894–95), during which three camels were captured and forcibly "conscripted" into the Imperial Japanese Army. Two years after the war, the camels were sent to Ueno Zoo as part of its popular "live-animal war trophy" (*senrihin dōbutsu*) exhibit. The opportunity for ethnic ego stroking was far from lost on some. "Foreign sources say that camels are actually depraved beasts," wrote one observer. "This is certainly true. If camels were people, they'd be just like the Chinese" (289). Japan's zoo inhabitants were hardest hit during the Pacific War. Because they were both in danger and a danger in and of themselves, captive animals were "mobilized" to do their part. The Ueno Zoo's two female elephants, Tonki and Hanako, were called upon by the Yasukuni Shrine, the ever-controversial memorial to the war dead, to "perform" for the benefit of grieving children who had lost their fathers. The elephants were also ordered to officiate at the memorial services of other military animals. Not even domestic animal populations were exempt from such displacements. One nationwide campaign called for pet "donations," rounding up dogs and cats and bludgeoning them to death so their fur could be used to line the coats of soldiers. Meanwhile, the Imperial Japanese Army was said to have treated its horses, which it called "living weapons," better than its own men (Itoh 2010, 28).

The most systematic disregard for nonhumans took place between August 1943 and May 1945, when the governor-general Ōdachi Shigeo ordered the disposal of animals in untold numbers. Starting with the zoos of Japan and eventually moving out into colonial territories across Korea, Taiwan, and Manchukuo, Ōdachi's order was all the more unusual for being a national policy. While similar exterminations were being carried out in other war-affected nations, these were always at the whim of local authorities taking matters into their own hands. Under the pretext of public safety, Japan had already "destroyed a total of more than 300 popular animals well before the U.S. B-29 air strikes on major cities in the nation were anticipated" (8). So began an unprecedented liquidation that took many forms. Less popular animals were simply culled, destroyed, and fed to other animals, leaving the rest to be strangled, shot, poisoned, and, more often—like Japan's first Ueno Zoo victim, John the elephant—starved to death after his living quarters were repurposed by the Tokyo Park Section "to store five hundred coffins in case of calamitous death tolls of citizens from air raids" (43). Incidentally, when the expected B-29s deployed their incendiaries over Tokyo on April 3, 1945, the only part of the Ueno Zoo to sustain any damage of note was the very room from which John had been evicted.

A rarely acknowledged side effect of these killings was the trauma suffered by those forced to carry them out. Extant testimonies from zoo workers reveal that looking those animals in the eyes was often the most difficult part of their task. Some workers were tormented by recurring nightmares. So powerfully did they haunt them that when, in 1952, the Ueno Zoo became home to a new pair of hippopotami, veteran keepers found themselves, much to the ignorance of an elated public and zoo officials, reliving memories of the ones they were ordered to starve during the war. Some zookeepers were known to have shed tears in private, while others held clandestine funeral services. Animals at private zoos (e.g., Higashiyama Zoo and Hanshin Park Zoo) fared only slightly better. Because municipally owned flagship operations like Ueno were better equipped to handle the financial burdens of animal extermination, private zoos saw no other recourse than to relocate their animals as best they could. As far as safety was concerned, the disposals were entirely unnecessary. Not one animal in Japan was killed as a result of Allied attacks.

The Ueno Zoo exemplifies what Ian Miller (2013, 3) calls Japan's "ecological modernity," connoting a "doubled process of intellectual separation and social transformation" to challenge scripts of modernity that assert a clear division between human and animal societies. As "a theater of Anthropocene culture in Japan" that "has gone from a place where captive wild animals were framed as exotic reflections of nature's ferociousness or fecund abundance to one where the animals themselves appear as figures of loss, disappearance, and extinction" (9), the Ueno Zoo hides its animal histories by displaying them in plain sight, clothing the disease of the past in the threads of the here and now. Japanese literature is the outerwear of that ensemble.

In her discussion of biological and environmental toxicity in Japanese literature, Christine Marran speaks of "obligate storytelling," which seeks to highlight materiality and any literary apparatus describing it. Obligate storytelling "not only admits the affectivity of other organisms but also seeks ways to illustrate that affectivity" (2017, 48). Animals serve as one of many possible such poles to which meaning might be attracted. She cautions tendency toward "a rigid divide between human civilization and nature that denies or represses our reality" because of "just how fundamental the natural world is to producing cultural and political collectivities" (10). The proliferation of postwar fiction proved this tendency toward incorporation of the synthetic and the organic. Among other unimaginable events, the atomic bombings of Hiroshima and Nagasaki brought about collapses in which human bodies were disintegrated into the same molecular matter of which all nature consists. The desire to narrate that contradictory state of separation from life and oneness with creation motivated many pens to even more pages.

After World War II, Nakamura Mitsuo declared that Japanese literature continued either as political novels or inwardly focused character studies (Holt 2016, 28). Both genres concern themselves with robust delusions of supremacy in proportion to humanity's distance from nature. Masaoka Shiki openly lamented this distance for casting an unresolvable shadow across many authorial quests for "Japaneseness" (Beichman 1986, 102). Later, Shiga Naoya would struggle to find in nature a wellspring of artistic creativity as translated through the seer's stone of "wisdom." Developing one's mind through the written word was a way of reconnecting to an Edenic state that had since been lost (Ueda 1976, 89-90). Natsume Sōseki, by contrast, saw nature as inimitable, while Mishima Yukio claimed nature could only be depicted fictionally because it was impossible to grasp except through metaphor.

Though Japan was no stranger to interpretations of human nature as moral acts (see Ōe 1996), it was not until the late twentieth century that philosophies of human–animal relations reached a saturation point in the context of popular literature and, through that transformation, planted a rich crop of productive error. Ōmura Eishō (2009) observes that Japan's falling birthrate had a direct impact on interest in pet keeping, by which new organic networks of social relations came into play and allowed animals into formerly taboo domestic spaces. The shift from patriarchal households to what Ōmura calls a fluid "neo-familism" allowed a different outlook on the ephemerality of relationships so that when loved ones died, people looked at them less as objects of awe and more as souls to whom intimate feelings were directed, cushioning the slow blow of mortality. Such concerns over animal keeping and national sovereignty, broken families, and death are ever swirling through the lives and actions of *Promises*.

Putting a Collar on Anxiety

The underlying tension of the film is reproductive in nature. Because the young Akari must learn to displace her love onto a dog groomed to replace her mother, she is constantly faced with a tangible figurehead of the role she must one day replicate when she has children of her own. In 2007, the year of the film's production, Japan had just witnessed the most dramatic drop in national birth rates since their initial decline in the mid-1970s. The fears raised by this information were only compounded by some staggering, if fatalistic, projections, some of which foresaw Japan dwindling to a population of only forty million by the year 2100. Not coincidentally, the film takes place in Hakodate, a small port city in Hokkaido.

Among Japan's more rapidly shrinking metropoles, Hakodate was an ideal place in which to explore the theme of fading populations. Since 1995, Hakodate had seen its numbers drop from 318,308 to around 280,000 by the time of the film's release. The decline of Hakodate's commercial industries led to an economic crisis in the 1970s, when its citizens began moving to the suburbs, emptying the inner city of half its residents. While the more visible agglomerations around satellite cities like Tokyo and Osaka seem to attract a continual influx of people and development, most others in Japan have followed Hakodate's lead. When we first meet Akari, she is heading up the Mount Hakodate Ropeway, staring down at the city proper as she looks to her past and to the dog who made it unforgettably rich. This ascent is a pivotal image for singling out Akari as one body from the invisible multitudes below. The goal now forced upon her is to repopulate this figureless cityscape. As an adult, Akari is calm and collected, keen to life's hardships and all the stronger for them. In her lives a story that, until now, was only hers, though cinema allows her to edit it in her favor. By the end of her childhood, time has ceased to exist altogether, stuck as we are tracing the question mark of Akari's open-ended future.

While *Promises* may not fulfill the standard definition of melodrama, its reproductive leanings trigger melodramatic elements. Since the war, Japanese cinema has become inundated with "mother narratives" under the "sense that traditional family structures were being lost" (Wada-Marciano 2009, 20), and *Promises* recasts these tropes through an interspecies lens. Not unlike the canonical maternal melodramas, which employ the "device of devaluing and debasing the actual figure of the mother while sanctifying the institution of motherhood"

(Williams 1984, 3), *Promises* renders its female characters (Socks included) as sympathetic conduits for present-day concerns. Yet where in maternal melodramas those concerns centered around democratization, the aporia of modernization is now clearly embodied in the birth rate scare. The socially and politically constructed alterity of Japanese bodies so often highlighted in modern cinema has now been displaced onto the bodies of animals.

Nonhuman subjects provide an ideal compromise between the realist approach and the excess of melodrama. Dispossessed of intelligible language while unconditionally invested in our well-being, animals smooth over the errors of their human counterparts even as they productively underline them. Their lack of language becomes symptomatic, yet in their silence, animals may be shown to express far more than their human counterparts. The melodramatic space is also one which, in being historically specific, contradictorily erases its past, just as Akari has done by retelling what she wants us to see and hear. The only way for Akari's mother to achieve any influence is to succumb to the dying body from which it issues. The only one resigned to Fumiko's imminent death is Fumiko herself, who, though silent on the issue, accepts her fate with a smile for the sake of her family.

When confronted with her mother's absence, Akari retreats into isolation and fear. She copes by latching on to Socks as a figurehead of lost parenthood before rejecting her in pursuit of self-sufficiency. Akari lacks the stability of human relationships. She puts her energy into the zoo, where she surrounds herself with "nonobjects" whose well-being, while therapeutic for giving her a social purpose, is essentially passive. In such a setting, she can reform herself as often as she likes.

Mothers in melodrama are said to be either angelic or monstrous. *Promises* embraces both archetypes. Being close to death, Fumiko expresses the angelic through her calm resignation. In displacing her maternity on Socks, she becomes monstrous. Mothers also qualify as what the film scholar Mitsuhiro Yoshimoto calls the "lacking subject," by which he means that which "does not act according to its own will but acts following something or someone" (cited in Wada-Marciano 2009, 24). Socks is a paradoxical substitute, emphasizing the maternal lack while filling it with unconditional attention. Similarly, the melodramatic family is one in which power has been "displaced and confined within a patriarchal family" (Yoshimoto 1993, 105–6). Such power is unobtainable in *Promises* (as one frightened of the maternal, Yūichi makes for a poor patriarch). Additionally, melodramatic films often have no discernible villain, an invisible other. In *Promises*, the invisible villain is Fumiko's disease. Without it, she cannot be a victim.

One also wonders why Yūichi waited until Socks was dying before disclosing Fumiko's paintings. Was this Fumiko's dying wish? Will this not brand Akari with guilt for the rest of her life? Is not the film her trauma narrative? And why does Fumiko consciously place this burden on Akari? In her parents' attempt to shield Akari from harm, they have subjected her to it tenfold. In response to those who believe the melodramatic is dead, Yoshimoto (1993, 121) suggests it has become unconscious. Hence the apparent innocence of these characters, whose motivations slip from the viewer's grasp. Consequently, most important in melodrama is how social change must be understood behind closed doors, expressed by the privacy of Akari's guilt, which is never disclosed to us. This privacy brings us full circle to Mulvey's evergreen point on looking. Through its misalignment with lived experience, the melodramatic is enhanced by the participation of animals whose inner lives are only as active as our own.

Because recollections of childhood are selective by default, the dog's body becomes a space where Akari's continues unseen and unheard. Akari's desire reunites with an abandoned past and through her willingness to produce children as signs of a hopeful future. Though child-rearing practices have become more refracted through technology, women like Akari continue to bear the weight of daily life. Her mother behaves as she must but is given an out through death and through her legacy in the Ten Promises.

Promises hides behind a scrim of animal empathy to justify the mistreatment of women as subhuman. Just as the "image" of women is seen as false in contrast to a stable reality of male design, so are animals seen as transient companions in a stable reality of human design. Akari's individuation is built on Fumiko's absence and on Socks's selfless ability to provide therapy for her human family. Socks presents a corporeal alternative to, if not a narcissistic extension of, the absent mother, which is why Akari does not weep for her mother's passing until her catharsis in the film's only visualized death scene. Like the camera, we are barred from lingering on Fumiko's convalescence yet are bid to watch Socks's prolonged death without reprieve.

Looking into the Mirror

At the end of his career, the director Kurosawa Akira criticized the film industry for pandering to market trends and for remaking the same kinds of films over and over again. "If a movie about a cat does well," he quipped, "they make one about a dog" (quoted in Richie 2001, 214). In looking at *Promises*, however, we find that such films are never about the animal but about the humans they foil. The true protagonists are the ideologies they catalyze, their true themes the productive errors they bring to light. *Promises* is as much situational and emotional as it is cultural and time specific.

Dogs can heal us in ways a line of doctors never could. Yet when that healing comes at the expense of a dog's well-being, how far can we milk the animal's patience for our gain? The answer of *Promises* is: As much as your hearts desire. Socks never *needs* attention, yet she is constantly portrayed as one *lacking* Akari's unconditional love. Akari has a life of her own to live. Surely, she cannot structure it around an animal she will outlive many times over. In addition to leaving Socks in an eternal state of unfulfillment, Akari's neglect perpetuates the invisibility of women's work. Hence the posthumous revelation of Fumiko's art, the brief montage of Akari's training at the zoo (portraying her only as an apprentice and never as a capable professional), Yūichi's failure to take on domestic duties in his wife's absence (and Akari's seamless adoption of the same), and the intense emotional labor provided by Socks herself. In bringing to light the agency of these acts and our inability to control them completely, we undermine an already-tenable authority.

Among the many memorable shots in *Promises* is one in which Socks regards herself in a mirror. As we watch Socks watching herself, we realize she is as illusory as her reflection. She is that mirror, giving back the moral expectations invested in her canine body. No other position for Socks is possible—her depth is directly proportional to her devotion to Akari. Toussenel would be proud. As a moral boon to her immediate family and, by extension, to humankind, Socks *must* be devoid of personality to the point where she becomes behavior incarnate, each action imbued with a didactic message. On the one hand, there is affirmation of animal sentience in a companion who cares unconditionally for Akari. On the other, Socks has never known the mother she is meant to replace. It makes sense that Akari would first encounter Socks through that backyard chase, as the dog becomes the moving target of a pursuit that will continue for the rest of her life. Only as an object of private conquest does Socks gain meaning. Only through guilt can she be loved.

Part 2: Animalizing the Disabled

> "In a warlike and restless clan . . . the sicklier man
> may have occasion to be alone, and may therefore
> become quieter and wiser; the one-eyed man will
> have one eye the stronger; the blind man will see
> deeper inwardly, and certainly hear better. To this
> extent, the famous theory of the survival of the fit-
> test does not seem to me to be the only viewpoint
> from which to explain the progress of strengthen-
> ing of a man or of a race."
> —Friedrich Nietzsche (1996, 138–39)

There is a thorn in the paw of Friedrich Nietzsche's aphorism: Disability
must be exceptional to serve as a baseline for progress. In this instance,
he is guilty of the sort of tokenism that continues to haunt disability discourse today. His comparatives—"stronger," "more deeply," "sharper"—
read like the laundry list of a model minority sympathizer. Despite a
gallant attempt to "deploy the power of difference against cultures that
would make outcasts of disabled people" (Mitchell and Snyder 2000, 67),
Nietzsche risks polishing the master's tools in the process. Nevertheless,
his critique illuminates a persistent phenomenon. Not only are disabled
people relegated to the margins, but they are also encouraged to hold
those margins close as an identity. Only then can they be welcomed back
into the fold as exemplars of perseverance. Disability is "integral" insofar
as it is assimilated into "a norm that supports the perception of disability as an alien or exceptional condition" (Stiker 1999, xi). The allowance
of disabled people into nondisabled contexts offsets the need for social
change. Symbols and representations of disability undergo constant
reformation, sometimes even decay (Miles 2000, 616). Nietzsche is ill-
equipped to address this reformation.

Existing exit strategies from this quagmire leave much to be desired.
Governmental solutions rest on a medical model of disability, which
"emphasizes individual incapacity and medical authority, leaving little room for the expertise derived from a disabled person's embodied
experience" (Stevens 2013, 161). Few places have held to the medical
model more explicitly than modern Japan, where one major step in
this direction was the 1949 Law for the Welfare of Physically Disabled
Persons. Enacted for the benefit of World War II veterans, it came only
in direct response to demand from the disabled sector and not out of
any apparent interest in the establishment of support networks at a
time when disabled people felt physically and emotionally dependent

on blood relatives and were barred from achieving "full independence" (Hayashi and Okuhiro 2009, 423). The law's well-meaning provisions fueled the need for direct channels of assistance. Legislators of the 1960s responded by providing "residential institutions." These, too, back-fired, resulting in "a life of segregation and obedience, without privacy" (393–94). Disabled people had been shifted from one mode of confinement to another, pulled away from potential outreach into sometimes unsanitary, neglectful conditions.

Despite continued welfare attention, critics such as Yōda Hiroe remain wary of the advances made in disability rights, claiming Japan's social welfare system is myopically concerned with "rehabilitation" over "reintegration," exhibits overreliance on medicalization, and continues to leave disabled people in dependent positions (see Stevens 2013, 16–17). One problem rampant in, though by no means unique to, Japan is that "people with physical disabilities are seen to require concessions no more onerous than wheelchair ramps, guide dogs, Braille signage and so on" (75). Such narrow-mindedness carries a torch of outdated thinking and means thousands of disabled people in Japan remain woefully underrecognized.

A less obvious wrinkle in the Nietzschean stance on disability is that only humans are privy to its transformative powers. Case in point: Quill, a guide dog whose staunch determination invited the sympathies of a nation in ways not witnessed since Hachikō. The guide dog, for its part, is a placeholder "for the ways in which disability becomes understood (and often feared) as a potential identity for everyone" (McHugh 2011, 31) and, like Hachikō, offsets deeply rooted discriminations. Quill's experiences exemplify how disability itself can function as a "narrative prosthesis." This term comes from the book of the same name by David Mitchell and Sharon Snyder, who use it to describe the literary device by which disability becomes a stepping-stone toward grander moral conclusions that ultimately apply only to those considered "whole." Through this process, "disabled characters have been consistently received by readers and viewers as isolated cases" (Mitchell and Snyder 2000, 29). Therein lies the central danger of disability tales: They are empathic black holes that affect minimal, fleeting change in the everyday.

The literary guide dog fulfills practical and abstract functions by shedding light on a unique dependency while bolstering human superiority through the power and ingenuity of guide dog training. The guide dog is a living badge of honor, an advertiser of purpose that bolds the norms behind its institution. To better situate those norms, I begin by sketching a brief history of blindness that couches Quill's biography before offering some theoretical context. Ultimately, we will see that the guide dog—despite being a fully cognizant actor in all of this—comes to be treated as an expendable variable of emotional transference by means of which those who produce disability narratives in the popular arena are able to capitalize on animal utility.

Seeing Japan for What It Is

Visual impairment has a checkered past in Japan. During the Tokugawa period, blind people were typically coerced into the arts, primarily as itinerant minstrels known as *biwa-hōshi*. As such, they took on circumscribed value, especially among the feudal lords who exploited them as clandestine messengers thought able to communicate with the dead. Blind artists contributed greatly to Japan's aesthetic evolution—as keepers of oral traditions, accompanists on the theatrical stage, religionists, and the like—and enhanced the creature comforts of the nobility retaining them as masseuses and entertainers. *Biwa-hōshi* were not handed their social status by a higher power but forged a status for themselves through clever personal mythologies (Miles 2000, 612). Their position became so great that so-called blind guilds (*tōdō-za*) prevented blind artists from falling into the "special status" category of outcastes until those safety nets came undone in 1871 (Groemer 2001, 373). Furthermore, blind female spirit mediums, or *itako*, of the northeastern provinces were believed to possess inherent shamanistic abilities. Fears of proximity to death relegated *itako* to the margins, where they developed an insular subculture. The *itako* also gained viable social status, if only locally, by virtue of their supposed ability to see in ways the sighted could not, all of which served to reinscribe the notion of blindness as a gateway condition. The "otherness" of their impairment validated the supernatural acts with which they came to be associated.

In 1872, the Meiji government established a compulsory educational system that excluded blind people, clinching their status as keepers of an oral archive and as acupuncturists and Chinese herbalists. Only when the Fundamental Law of Education was passed in 1947 did education for blind children become compulsory. Under the new law, they were placed in special classrooms, isolated from their nondisabled counterparts. Children in such institutions were ranked by the severity of their impairments, resulting in an arbitrary hierarchy of disabilities. The "least impaired" among them became favorites of teachers and staff.

These children "then adopted an 'elite' attitude, and considered themselves superior to residents with more severe impairments" (Hayashi and Okuhiro 2009, 395). Such feelings of superiority were specific to the institutional environments that fostered them and in no way equipped students with the armor necessary to fend off the "specific norms of communication and consciousness" being anchored and reproduced in such schools (Whyte and Muyinda 2007, 294).

As recently as the early 1980s, "Japanese society did not perceive the confining of disabled persons in institutions for life as a human-rights violation" (Hayashi and Okuhiro 2009, 391). Neither did this confining stop at the institutional level, as many were "funnelled without distinction into low-paying jobs, instead of being encouraged to seek further training to reach their full employment potential" (Stevens 2013, 81). So underwritten, their marginality as human beings only grew with time. Ongoing discrimination against the blind has since led to the formation of local clubs providing networks of helpers for various activities.

Following social integration in the 1970s alongside a nascent Disability Rights Movement, the 1980s saw an increase in the number of disabled people transitioning into independent living. The number of, and attention paid to, personal attendants also grew. This led to the formation of the Japan Council on Independent-Living Centers in 1991 and, with the help of advocates from the United States, a rise in guide dog numbers. Lack of funding, resources, and qualified trainers prevented this luxury from becoming widely available. Times of crisis have been the greatest mirrors for the inadequacies of this legislation. Partially instigated by an inability to accommodate the blind in the wake of 3/11, October of that same year (2011) saw an unprecedented change in the welfare service system for the blind, including nationwide standardization of safety escorts trained to assist in daily tasks, as well as a marked rise in the use and availability of guide dogs.

Guide dog training came to Japan in 1938, but it was not until 1967 that the Japanese Guide Dog Association was established at the Ministry of Welfare's behest. Another important development came in 1973 when Japanese National Railways instituted its Service Standards for Passengers, which allowed visually impaired passengers to be accompanied by their guide dogs on trains. In 2002, the Law Concerning Service Dogs for People with Disabilities was passed by the National Diet, giving guide dog owners greater access to public facilities and transportation. In spite of these advances, the stress levels of those with guide dogs have been shown to be higher than those without them

(Matsunaka and Koda 2008, 303). Some establishments, restaurants in particular, continue to refuse service to any customer accompanied by an animal on the grounds of sanitation. As Sadakazu Shimojiyu, the head of the Kansai Guide Dogs for the Blind Association, told the *Independent* on February 4, 1993, "Up to now, we have been promoting guide dogs to blind people. From now on, we need to promote understanding of guide dogs among seeing people." Steps in this direction have taken many forms, notably as a Tokyo discrimination awareness rally held in honor of International Guide Dog Day in April 2012.

Guide dogs as a Japanese cultural phenomenon in the last decade can be traced to a single book and its adapted film (as detailed in the following section). The guide dog lends specific and undeniable visuality to the condition of blindness while providing the same function of displacement. The guide dog compensates for impairment and takes on the possibility of sight through substitution. More importantly, the guide dog opens up a line of communication between user and dog, dog and society, and society and user. This triangle would seem to enable reintegration of the blind into the social matrix, with the dog acting as a mediator between worlds. Such has not been the case.

Feathering the Quill

On July 8, 1998, in Kyoto, Nii Isamu and his wife Mitsuko bade farewell to a special companion. Quill, a Labrador retriever guide dog who lived a full twelve years, died in the quiet comfort of his foster family's home. His death was such a blow that, five years later, a book of letters honoring the faithful dog was published in his remembrance (Ishiguro 2003). What was it about this single canine that put a finger on the pulse of the national ethos? Our first clue can be found in the proliferation of dogs in the mainstream Japanese literary market. Since becoming something of a posthumous celebrity, Quill has sparked interest in marginalized canines—service dogs, disabled dogs, and neglected or abused dogs—as paragons of moral virtue.

At the time of Quill's death, less than one thousand guide dogs were actively registered in Japan, with nearly five thousand hopeful users on the waiting list for a canine assistant (Ishiguro 2001). The statistic fares little better today and is a contributing factor to the paltry 30 percent employment rate of Japan's 350,000 blind. This segregation conforms to the strictures of times past in spite of a legislative crawl toward progress. When Quill's story was told in Ishiguro Kengo's docu-novel

Quill: The Life of a Guide Dog in 2001, it flicked a raw nerve. Ishiguro's book—
a mélange of interviews, photographs (courtesy of Akimoto Ryōhei), and
dramatization—presents Quill as a hero. Yet what is, on the surface,
touching proof of dedication harbors dire messages along with the
good, questioning notions of purity, human–animal relations, and public perceptions of the blind in tandem.

June 25, 1986. Quill is born in Tokyo. Like Japan's bubble economy,
the young Quill is preparing for a period of intense growth and sudden
downfall. For now, his destiny is unknown. His original owner harbors
dreams of breeding Labs of "guide dog caliber" and consults Kyoto-
based handler Tawada Satoru, the man responsible for breeding Quill's
mother—a common house pet—with a guide dog of reputable pedigree.
The book makes it a point to stress that Quill and his siblings have
"guide dog blood" (*mōdōken ni tekishiteiru kettō*) in their veins (22), weav-
ing a eugenic thread throughout.

Purebreds are preferred for service work, as they tend to act more
predictably during training. Thus, purity is transformed via the canine
body from an ideal into a norm. For a blind person to function in society, they must put trust in the vessel of purity society has provided for
that purpose. This has the hypocritical effect of reinforcing the impurity
of the impairment. Only after much imploring does Tawada agree to
take one puppy for training and send over a colleague to evaluate the
litter's behavioral cues. Successful guide dogs display certain personality
traits early on, and it is these Tawada and his associates look for in any
potential guide dog. Docility matters above all, for it conveys a dog who
will not be distracted by everyday sights and sounds. Quill is singled out
for his quiet attitude and for never developing "the competitive streak
of his siblings" (17).

Quill bears a streak of a different kind in the form of a dark spot on
his side, a genetic defect that belies his subpure lineage. Rather than
be seen as such, the spot is claimed as a good omen, "a message to the
world that he was destined to touch people's lives" (197). The blemish valorizes and objectifies his potential, performing just the sort of
exceptionalism Nietzsche proposes. As the tainted runt of the litter,
his reserved nature is configured as destiny. It is significant that Quill
is so marked, as if he would *have* to be to serve with such devotion,
even after his retirement. Quill's blemish is explicitly remarked upon
when the forty-three-day-old puppy is welcomed into the Niis' lives.
At first, the spot confuses Mitsuko, who assumes someone must have
deliberately put it there.

As Quill's designated "puppy walkers," Mitsuko and her husband are tasked with acclimating him. So begins Ishiguro's attempt to inculcate readers in the text's anthropocentric concerns. While there is some description of the dog's movement from home to home, the focus is on the emotional well-being of his caretakers. In this vein, the Niis are described as a couple whose "former pet collie had been like a child to them, and her death had left a gaping hole in their lives" (51). Say the Niis, "We knew the dog would be heading off for training just when we were beginning to bond. But we also felt it would be easier knowing the dog was going on to bigger and better things than having to lose a dog we had lived with for much longer" (51). That the Niis see a causal relationship between "bigger and better things" and an animal's utility is understandable given that Quill is being groomed as a prosthesis for a human need. They are doing something positive for the nation. In a telling aside, they make it a point to talk about the two guide dogs they raised in the past. They are proudest of the second because she and her user together climbed Mounts Fuji and Haku and even completed the formidable Kannon 100 Circuit. The patriotic fervor of this testimony is as blatant as it is briefly noted. So deep is their faith in Quill that when the time comes to relinquish him to the training center, "Their hearts were close to bursting as they thought back on what a rambunctious, but intelligent puppy he had been" (77). This blend of childlike and sagacious qualities is soon to be tested.

Trainer Tawada is known as "The Magician" and is thought to be "more canine than human," making him something of a dog whisperer (62). His status as such pegs him as an outsider, as someone like the feared *itako* who shuttles to and from a world incomprehensible to the rest of us. Tawada recalls Quill as being "unremarkable" when he was first brought to the training facility, even as he praises the dog's incredible obedience, which "set him apart from the rest. He never let his personality get in the way" (94). Tawada notes the initial difficulties of training Quill, stubborn from the first: "He might have been a puppy, but he behaved more like a middle-aged man!" (86). Clearly, Quill is being held to the same standards to which he will one day accede. In anticipation of criticism, Tawada is clear about the dogs' enjoyment, saying, "Dogs love to work, so they find the guide dog training, and by extension being loyal to their user, rather fun" (85).

Meanwhile, Watanabe Mitsuru, a native of nearby Kameoka, has been vehemently against the idea of a guide dog since losing his sight at the age of forty-two. And yet, after a period of intense mutual training with

Quill, Watanabe is able to live independently again. "He's more than a dog," says the convert, "he's a real companion" (138). After two bliss-ful years, tragedy strikes when Watanabe's kidneys begin to fail, leav-ing Quill stuck in the training center kennel. For three more years, the dog wallows in depression, after which a tearful reunion leads to a final walk together. Watanabe dies one week later. Considering the strength of their relationship, Tawada foresees only difficulty in pairing Quill with another "user" (as the Japanese parlance would have it). He finally decides to retire Quill from service and tout him instead as a social wel-fare ambassador. In this capacity, Quill averages ten demonstrations a year. Children are blindfolded at these events and led through an obsta-cle course, teaching them what it feels like to trust an animal. In a nation where the blind live in the shadows, Quill brings valuable learning to light and earns due media attention. When the Niis catch wind of this, they begin following him around, if only to glimpse the memorable canine who brought so much joy to their lives. They notice he is getting sluggish and ask the training center if he might spend his remaining days at their home. Tawada agrees to this unorthodox request. As Quill lies dying, Isamu tells the dog, "And when you get to Heaven, you tell them loud and clear that your name is Quill Nii!" (193). He is their kin, after all.

Quill is about disability. Does it concede to the usual protocol? Susan McHugh (2011, 32) claims that "guide-dog fictions directly confront the negative image of a blind man led astray by (and consequently like) a dog." In this respect, the book succeeds bittersweetly. On the one hand, Watanabe's turnaround from curmudgeon to humanitarian speaks of something transformative in the human–dog relationship and echoes Rod Michalko's (1998) assertion that the quality of a blind person's life is only as good as the individual makes it out to be. Quill validates personal triumph in the absence of foreseeable hope, a stepping stone toward a breakthrough. Such is the power of biography to challenge the ableist paradigm.

Tobin Siebers, invoking the feminist-queer concept of "masquerade," criticizes the need for overt visual markers of "disability" (2011, 102). In the same way heterosexuality may be compulsory, so does able-bodiedness function in Quill as the unwavering norm to which both Watanabe and Quill must bow if they are to navigate the social landscape as fluidly as they do. Despite the communicative potential for masquerade, it comes with a price: "Many representations of people with disabilities . . . use nar-rative structures that masquerade disability to benefit the able-bodied public and to reinforce the ideology of ability. Human interest stories display voyeuristically the physical or mental disability of their heroes, making the defect emphatically present, often exaggerating it, and then wiping it away by reporting how it has been overcome, how the heroes are 'normal,' despite the powerful odds against them" (111). Quill functions in precisely this way—which is to say, as the surrogate hero in place of his feeble user. Each serves to solidify a normativity that transcends them both. The most useful guide dog is one who assesses the situation and looks for differences (e.g., in height between walking surfaces) to avoid danger. In Watanabe's assessment, "Quill has reminded me of how a person should walk" (Ishiguro 2001, 197). Quill is a blank slate for the anthropocentric cast of his employment. A nationalistic subtext secures the connection between such thinking and a collective consciousness. By mediating between Watanabe's formerly sheltered life and newfound compassion, guide dogs like Quill are empowering Japan's population, one citizen at a time.

The fact that Quill's entire life was so well documented in still images—portraying even his birth and death—gives his tale a voyeuristic quality, making Quill's distinguishing mark that much louder. It elevates his loyalty to a matter of national identity over breeding. Along these lines, in his afterword to the text, Ishiguro puts out a call for financial and volunteer resources, framing the guide dog shortage as a question of human labor while implicitly claiming it as a chance for Japan to "catch up" to the West in its personal and technological attention to disabilities of all kinds.

In a time when skin color is still hegemonized as a marker of race and ethnicity, disability is still essentially about looking. Consequently, the visuality of disability frames a question in need of answering: "What do we 'see' when we experience someone using a wheelchair or someone who is blind or when someone tells us they have a learning disability? Typically, what we 'see,' is a problem. But what sort of a problem and thus what sort of a solution do we perceive?" (Titchkosky and Michalko 2012, 136). Akimoto's accompanying photographs—and, by extension, the director Sai's 2004 screen adaptation—have made a bigger impact than the text. The adorability factor of the film goads attention away from the text's ideological pitfalls and provides an escapist promise of humanity's inherent goodness. By assuaging yet embodying fears of impermanence, the dog becomes a mechanism of levity in a nation still reeling from a string of earthquakes, tsunamis, and nuclear meltdowns.

Since the release of Sai's film, the guide dog has become the symbol par excellence of the Disability Rights Movement in Japan. In a thesis on the same, Wenwen Zhong (2011) divides the humans in Quill's milieux into three groups: elites (trainers), visually impaired persons, and the general public. The expertise of Quill's trainers is portrayed as something other than human, requiring a certain crossing over to flourish. Tawada inhabits two worlds, and neither of them fully. This is not to say this story has had no positive ramifications. The great success of the film, in particular, garnered Tawada and the Japanese Guide Dog Association much in the way of media coverage, resulting in a surge of public donations, as well as visits from celebrities and members of the Japanese royal family. The film was also instrumental in demystifying the relationship between humans and guide dogs.

Yet even the rainbow bears a scar. In the same way Hachikō, once the embodiment of national ethos in a time of great uncertainty, "has become a nostalgic symbol that promotes local commerce" (Ambros 2012, 190), so has Quill provoked just enough sympathy for the blind to feel that adequate attention has been paid. With confirmation and mental cataloging of that sympathy comes greater distance from it. Equally problematic is the fact that the book's construction as a documentarian (read: visual) object marks it as a product for the sighted alone. It, too, must abide by ableist rules of publishing, marketing, and distribution, such that the end effect flips by as ephemerally as Quill's life on the printed page.

Quill in Theory

Michel Foucault famously said that "[a] normalizing society is the historical outcome of a technology of power centered on life" (1990, 144). Disability effectively corroborates his thinking on this point. The divisiveness of biopower *creates* human subjects. The dark side to this telos is that biopower makes impairments seem natural against the "juridico-discursive" norms in which they are situated (see Tremain 2005, 10). If one can imagine that individuality, per se, is constructed by the norms of which it is composed, then one can also imagine that disability, insofar as it "belongs" to the individual it "afflicts," is a norm unto itself. It bears noting that the vast majority of people with disabilities or impairments are not born with them. Those who develop disabilities later in life envision themselves before and after those turning points, stressing that "becoming disabled not only alters our physical state, but may also alter our conception of time and life course progression" (Iwakuma 2001, 223). This is why narrations of disability tend to be so transparent. Quill's message feels objectively moral, a simple wisdom through which its cookie-cutter morals bake up all the sweeter.

The skeletal outline of justice presented in *Quill* is troubling. For even as the book shores up latent concerns about the segregation of disability, it cannot withstand the flood of denial that keeps it from standing tall. As an educational ambassador, Quill is an illusory subject of justice because, as an animal, he cannot be a "framer of contracts" (Nussbaum 2006, 335). That is, he cannot define the parameters of his legal and social stations. Though dogs and cats have become increasingly accepted as family members, the bonds of the family unit no longer carry the same precontractual weight they once did. It is for this reason that Quill's "true" family is to be found neither in the company of his birth mother nor even of Watanabe but with the elderly couple who taught him about this world and who stayed with him as he slipped over into the next. Quill can be no arbiter of social change because his legal status is forever ambiguous.

Still, change exists all around him. Wherever Quill goes, he makes an unforgettable impression, what Gilles Deleuze would call "impersonal singularity," whereby forces that exist outside the body precede the self while also being integral to the self. In this vein, James Overboe moves beyond the pathological model of impairment into a nuanced understanding that privileges generative life force over personhood and representation, treating the disabled body not as an "individual afflicted with impairments" but rather as a matrix of "singularities that affirm the impersonal life" (2012, 125). Normality is the construction from which the individual may be freed. Quill reminds us the disabled body is not "an entity that inhibits life" but one that "provides the vitality and is the basis for a life expressed" (124). Once again, the animal is sublimated by deference to a stubborn universalism.

In the context of *Quill*, blindness stands out by virtue of the dog's eventual absence. Watanabe can never overcome his condition; he can only wallow in it. Only once is he photographed in Ishiguro's book without Quill somewhere in frame, when he was first brought to the training facility grounds. His existence is indelibly marked by the dog, whose visual direction becomes part of his nonvisual compass. The persistence of their relationship reifies the "normate assumption that impairment cancels out other qualities, reducing the complex person to a single attribute" (Thomson 1997, 12). As a token of all blind people, Watanabe is pushed into a metanarrative that oversteps agency in favor of cultural representation.

The training of guide dogs ensures they know themselves in relation to humans and that they belong to a human pack. Quill is never in any doubt as to where he stands among others. Both the book and the film try their best to shift subjective primacy by drawing disparate elements together in such a way that blindness itself becomes the central protagonist, rendering the lives it affects as fleeting signals for its cause. In this manner, the author, photographer, and director redraw notions of utility and capability as parameters of social worth. The film's international traction is a productive error unto itself, for its assertion of capability and globalization gives rise to friction around problems of action, fairness, capacity, and personal life the film is unprepared to address.

Generic forms may offer a field of compromise in which to engage creatively and ethically with animals. Though, as McHugh (2011, 217) believes, "stories can (and indeed always) do more than represent selves at the expense of others," when para- and extratextual forces seem only to conspire against hope, one is challenged to find an antidote. Even if the point of narratology, as McHugh goes on to say, "is not to escape the stories so much as to reckon with the ways in which life continues only ever within them" (218), we must also ask: How does the *story* reckon *us*?

Seeing Is Unbelieving

In 2011, engineers from Japan's NSK Corporation unveiled their working prototype of a mechanical guide dog. Attractive in theory, the idea was grossly premature. How can blind users be expected to put their trust in machines? How might societies react to the sight of machine-assisted humans when they have yet to fully grapple with that of animal-assisted ones? Presumably, the technology would subsidize the need for biological guide dogs, but its existence would reframe guide dogs' fallibility in proportion to the time and money invested in them. Balancing the ways mobile and virtual technologies abstract the self through such avatars, the constructed canine gives social actors a focal point on which to project an ideal, completed self.

The implications are far-reaching. Robotic assistance affirms the currency of what Miryam Sas (2011, 57) calls "apparence" in the world, which is to say the degree to which one is noticeable directly correlates to the standards by which one is valued, recognized, and privileged. It is for this reason that "forms of representation matter to the development of theories of species life" (McHugh 2011, 218) and why stories like Quill's, owing to their popularity and archetypal structure, carry so much weight. There is something of a "desire to see more" in the promise of blindness (Sas 2011, 61), but it is transferred and romanticized by the sighted, who are the producers, targets, and consumers of such stories.

Because the disabled are "based in their bodies but not confined to flesh or its past perfect" and are concerned instead with their "future declension" (Miller 2011, 283), they have already broken through barriers of communication, waiting for the nondisabled to catch up. That said, "[t]he idea that individuals with physical, sensory or cognitive impairments all together form a class of 'the disabled' is a twentieth century invention" (Silvers 2010, 23). In the instance of *Quill*, it may not, as McHugh (2011, 219) suggests, behoove us to think of "molecular groupings" over "atomized individuals." Rather, disability is to be taken on its own terms and contextualized accordingly. Like the black-clad manipulators of Japanese puppet theatre, the purpose of guide dogs is often romanticized as disappearance when, if anything, that purpose is to be seen, to make obvious that the sighted are subject to forces of which they may be unaware yet cannot be unseen once noticed.

Part 3: Disabling the Animal

"Dogs are us, only innocent."
—Cynthia Heimel (cited in Lane 2007, 161)

On July 28, 2014, in the city of Saitama, a guide dog named Oscar was reportedly stabbed with a pronged object while walking his user, a sixty-one-year-old man, to work. Because guide dogs are trained to remain silent while on duty, it was only when a coworker noticed blood that Oscar's user became aware of the injury. By November, local investigators were struggling to piece the events together. After three months of solid investigation, and with no evidence of foul play to show for it, police remained tight-lipped about their suspicions. The supposed crime produced no witnesses, and security camera footage yielded nothing of consequence. In response to mounting public outcry, authorities enlisted the assistance of a reputable veterinarian, who concluded that Oscar had not been attacked but was suffering from pyoderma, a skin disease known for producing lesions that resemble stab wounds. Beyond seizing the incident for shock copy, the press cared little for the relationship between the man and his guide dog and chose to ignore the possible discriminations, which, like Oscar's wounds, might have oozed with the blood of a systemic problem. The misunderstanding of the dog's victimhood meant that once-outraged readers could forget about the social environment in which its reportage had played out. Oscar mattered only as a victim, never as a subject.

Traumality, in light of productive error, is effective for rethinking the parameters of animal entitlements and physiological thresholds and serves to dismantle assumptions founded on human superiority. It also reframes descriptions of animal trauma as displacements, which shield humans from confronting a fundamental inter-implicatedness. Likewise, guide dog users in Japan are socially displaced. As impaired individuals in need of prostheses, their attempts at (re)integration are only nominally successful once they gain the companionship of a service animal. If society sees blind people and their guide dogs as codependent, blind users can take that thinking further, as the absence of sight leaves them more open to physical permeability without ocular bias to dictate separations of bodies.

The original *Asahi Shimbun* article on the Oscar incident confirms this when it quotes his user as saying, "Oscar is part of my body. I cannot possibly forgive the assailant who stabbed him, which is equal to stabbing me. I'm afraid to go out at the thought of being targeted again." The fact that danger could come at any time from without threatens Oscar's user from within. He frames his relationship with the guide dog as one of transspecies assemblage, "an irreducibly different and unique form of subjectivity," as Cary Wolfe (2010, 141) has it, "neither *Homo sapiens* nor *Canis familiaris*, neither 'disabled' nor 'normal,' but something else altogether, a shared trans-species being-in-the-world constituted by complex relations of trust, respect, dependence, and communication." The relationship between humans and guide dogs is more than that; it is an existential symbiosis. Favoring the dog alone as victim shortchanges this symbiosis.

Oscar and his user are one entity, sharing life without the need for distinction. The traumality of Oscar's injury compels his user to publicly avow the nature of their relationship by outing himself as a "canine-human" in a society of "human-human" individuals. The press's instinct to cry foul suggests a desire to heighten the heroism of human intervention. The injured guide dog, as a marker of "outsiderness," baits aberrant criminals. The possible error of Oscar's injuries gives humans cause to oust one of their own—flagging the disabled as a weed in need of pulling. Oscar's puncture upsets boundaries between inside and outside, but the connective potential of this rupture is never cultivated. Recognizing the two as one would have instigated an inappropriate discussion, as proven by the apparent sense of relief when it was determined no crime had been committed, freeing readers from the mental labor of having to accept the hybridity of this relationship and allowing them to go on roaming networks of explicitly individuated species.

Acknowledgment of human–guide dog symbioses raises the question of whether problems related to guide dogs and their handlers are a simple fact of literature about them or a genre-specific consequence. To answer this, I look to the philosopher Martha Nussbaum (2006, 94) and her concept of the "species norm," a moral system whereby capacities are evaluated vertically rather than horizontally. Norms exist not only for nondisabled humans but also for those less than human (or less than able). These norms can be used as much to cut across boundaries between "higher" and "lower" as to reinforce their vertical arrangement. What distinguishes guide dogs is their grappling with, and redefinition of, species norms in relation to social conditions of which they are symptomatic.

Japanese guide dog literature consists almost entirely of actual guide dogs. Fictional representations are rare and geared mainly toward younger audiences. Guide dog literature for adults is dramatized for emotional impact, yet its archival feel makes it worthy of criticism as a marketable genre. I choose to evaluate guide dog literature, at least in terms of species norms, as a wholehearted campaign to reconceptualize human–animal relationships. If guide dog literature has the *opposite* effect of shoring up the divide between humans and animals, it is by no fault of its own but of the markets in which it is published, consumed, and adored as a paean to species norms. Nussbaum elaborates: "[T]he species norm . . . tells us what the appropriate benchmark is for judging whether a given creature has decent opportunities for flourishing. The same goes for nonhuman animals: in each case, what is wanted is a species-specific account of central capabilities (which may include particular interspecies relationships, such as the traditional relationship between the dog and the human), and then a commitment to bring members of that species up to that norm, even if special obstacles lie in the way of that" (365). Pervasive species norms serve as leveling mechanisms against the potential of guide dogs to activate productive errors, presenting social architects with blueprints for progressive change and explosives for the demolition of that change in equal measure. Species norms are ideals into which guide dogs and their users must fit if they are to attain validity as subjects who know their place. They are symbiotic only because guide dogs are assumed to "complete" a blind user's physical handicap in mimicry of ableist norms. The guide dog is nothing more than a conductor for a blind user's electricity of independence.

Japanese disability narratives favor form over content, fawning over displaced animality to keep categories separate. There is a sense that disabled people can only achieve integration by capitalizing on their inability to integrate—in other words, by "owning up" to their special status. Because they are seen to persevere *in spite of* being disabled, their disability remains an unwavering precondition for personal accomplishment. In the following sections, I sketch three such narratives and assess how their bridging of disability and animality reinforces their subhuman conditions and hints at overcoming them. From this, I paint a picture of traumality as an emotional force that nurtures sameness through difference, one by which inclusivity models of disability are shown to be assemblages of productive errors.

Wagging the Dog: The Case of Berna

Shioya Ken'ichi is the founder of Eye Mate, Inc., one of Japan's oldest guide dog associations. He has trained dozens of guide dogs in his lifetime, including the wounded Oscar, throughout his long career. His most famous clients are Gunji Nanae and her black Labrador, Berna. Born in the city of Takada (now Jōetsu) in Niigata prefecture, Gunji contracted Behçet's disease at the age of seventeen and was fully blind by twenty-seven. Her autobiographical *Berna's Tail* (*Beruna no shippo*) was published at the height of the pet boom in 1996. It chronicles the challenges of living and working with a guide dog but is, above all, about adaptation and steadfastness. When the reader first encounters Gunji, she has been relying on a white cane to get around for some time but finds it cumbersome. She dreams of having children, if only to have someone to care for her. Only then does she entertain what she calls a "desperate idea" (*zetsubō no omoi*): Why not get a guide dog? She calls Ken'ichi, who tells her, "If you can pet a stuffed animal, you can handle a real one" (Gunji 2002, 19).

Berna's Tail did for dogs what Anna Sewell's *Black Beauty* did for horses. In addition to addressing the challenges of empathizing with working animals, both authors share striking connections with disability. Gunji's trials as a blind woman acclimating herself to the freedoms afforded by her guide dog parallel to those of Sewell, who relied on horse-drawn transportation after suffering a permanent, crippling injury at age fourteen. But Gunji's introduction to Berna is a nerve-wracking moment, less because she must learn a new way of getting around and more because she has been deathly afraid of dogs since a traumatic childhood experience. The more she works with Berna, the more dovetailed she and the dog become. Gunji passes her graduation test and finds hard-won freedom in her newfound abilities. "It's easy to think that blind people simply rely on guide dogs to take them where they need to go, but this isn't the case," she elaborates. "Blind people must have their routes firmly in mind at all times . . . and dictate those routes through gestures and words" (61–62).

Gunji is a pioneer for documenting Japan's widespread resistance to guide dogs in the 1980s. When she first brings Berna home on the train, she is met with a station attendant who has never heard the term "guide dog." A crowd gathers. Says one, "Oh, a guide dog! I've seen those on TV." "What's a guide dog? Looks like your run-of-the-mill mutt to me," says another (54). As Gunji continues to face challenges when trying to eat out at restaurants or access public facilities, she encounters instances of kindness and understanding (67–70). As her confidence in Berna grows, so does people's acceptance of their partnership. And so, "the user's life depends on whether she can demonstrate the kind of love that requires people both to give dogs direction and at pivotal moments to honor their dogs' leadership" (McHugh 2011, 53). It is a relationship of survival by which the stakes of quotidian tasks take on heightened importance.

As is common in guide dog stories, Berna's declining health is a central plot point. When she is diagnosed with cataracts during a routine checkup at age nine, her veterinarian suggests that the dog retire. The irony of it all—a guide dog trained to help the blind becoming blind—throws Gunji into a panic. She cannot bear the thought of decommissioning Berna but also worries about working the dog in her condition. The vet assures her dogs are remarkable for being able to navigate familiar terrain even with poor eyesight, relying as they do on strengths in other faculties. The traumality of Berna's cancer diagnosis at age fourteen causes greater stress for Gunji, who finds strength in the dog's will to live. They go through a long and painful goodbye, during which time Berna's tail becomes her final means of able communication. Berna's tail is more than a title; it is a metonym for the dog herself, an emotional antenna so emblematic that the word "tail" (*shippo*) appears no fewer than thirty-two times in the text.

Berna's Tail broke ground by lending credence to the challenges of life with (and without) a guide dog. It forged new perspectives on the general public's willingness to accept disabled people as functioning members of society. Gunji's matter-of-fact approach sustained her through later tragedies, including the loss of her husband to liver cancer at age forty-nine and the death of her second guide dog, Garland, with whom she shared only fourteen months of companionship and who became the subject of two subsequent books. In 1995, Gunji befriended a third guide dog, Perilla, with whom she toured extensively for educational outreach. Her persistence won.

Disappearing Dog: The Case of Tarō

In late autumn of 1995, while walking through Buddhist temple grounds on the outskirts of Munakata City in Fukuoka prefecture, a concerned citizen came upon a box of puppies abandoned near a public toilet. Many dogs and cats had been left for dead at this very spot, and the woman had cared for nearly one hundred of them in the past year alone. Unable to bear the thought of euthanasia, she had made a practice of rehabilitating her discoveries and bringing them to the local Komori Animal Hospital for care and placement. Among them was the subject of *Day by Day with Tarō, the Disabled Dog* (*Shōgaiken Tarō no mainichi*). Sasaki Yuri's 2007 biography tells of how Tarō, born without defect, suffered a rare constellation of circulatory disturbances brought on by thrombosis and vascular disease that ate away most of his limbs, ears, and tail. Though not as extensively marketed as the exploits of Berna and Quill, Tarō's tale of survival made him an emblem of hope for those who dare doubt the power of will. And yet, a superficial engagement with disability lurks beneath Tarō's perseverance. His story and others like it serve a populist agenda, privileging unfettered emotional glitter over the darkness faced by disabled people in contemporary Japan.

Because Tarō was one of countless throwaway (*shobun*) pets destined to perish, one may read him in terms of vanishing. The image of his flesh-eating disease, which earns him the descriptor "the dog with an incomplete body," reifies the normalcy of a complete one. Despite managing to function in human society, Tarō's value as an animal is proportional to his usefulness. His brush with certain death is an affirmation of human life and the ideal of sentient expression that accompanies it. Unique about Tarō is the fact that, rather than assisting someone who is disabled, the dog is himself disabled. And yet, in the same way *Quill* drops the ball when it comes to critical reflection, Tarō's biography deflates the potential for cognitive refreshment in deference to an airily inspirational approach that ignores the reinscriptions of which it is a part.

Tarō's biography confirms the assumptions of normalcy that went into its production. For proof, one need only consider the book's obi, which reads: "By simply living a normal life, Tarō is bringing good cheer to all" (*Goku futsū ni ikite iru dake de, Tarō wa hito o genkizukete iru*). The obi further boasts the endorsement of Quill's biographer, Ishiguro. The very idea of a "normal life" is fraught with ableism, for it assumes a consensus understanding of its terms. In reinforcing that consensus, the book sets up expectations of the status quo before the front cover is even opened. Tarō is overdetermined by his aspiration to able-bodied–ness and in his mental surpassing of it.

This makes Sasaki's wholehearted attempts to place Tarō in dialogue with animal welfare all the more interesting. As the most recent of the three books detailed here, it has the benefit of hindsight. Sasaki goes into some depth about Japan's pet boom, to which she attributes a rising awareness of animal worth. As an abandoned stray who was, "against the fashion of the times, an utterly worthless mixed breed from the perspective of a trend-conscious society" (Sasaki 2007, 9), Tarō upsets the purebred paradigm of widespread pet keeping that was then still a recent cultural adoption. Despite Sasaki's dig at what she calls a "trend-conscious society" obsessed with designer breeds, clothing, and lifestyles, it is difficult to assess the strength of her critique when, a page earlier, she quotes Dr. Komori Taiji, who replaces one notion of purity with another when he praises Tarō for being a "genuine mixed breed" (*shōshinshōmei no zasshuken*). While *Day by Day with Tarō* may outline the pet boom as a skeletal context for true dog stories, its veneer of social awareness hides a conundrum: With the validity of animals' sentience comes an anxiety over neutralizing their subhuman status.

Bill Pollard distinguishes between two understandings of virtuous action: first as "a process of *reconstructing* prior workings, which were present, if only subconsciously, to the agent at the time of acting," and second as "a process of creatively *constructing* an account of how the agent's action in its immediately worldly context coheres with her overall world-view, motivations, projects and so on" (2003, 424, original emphases). Pollard's definition of virtuous action comes about through its lack of deliberation over reasons or possible outcomes.

Clea F. Rees and Jonathan Webber, however, argue that "this distinction between whether and how to act should be replaced with a distinction between initiating and modifying motivations" (2014, 89n). The pathology of rescue practiced in the above fits the former profile in both instances as impulsive actions given heroic meaning through reconstruction. This does not undermine the desires of its actors but nevertheless strokes the ego that may come with habitual animal rescue.

Seminal studies of altruism, including those by Samuel and Pearl Oliner (1988) and Kristen Renwick Monroe (1996), have drawn profiles of rescue through traumas of the Nazi Holocaust. The Oliners theorize distinct forms of motivation for rescue. Their major contribution to this debate is a concept they call "normocentric" rescue, the motivations of which are tied to group behavior or self-enhancement. In that same line of discourse, Philip P. Hallie sees the act of selfless rescue not as one of brute force but of "undramatic compassion and hospitality" (1997, 235). I detect a hybrid of these motivations at work behind the traumalities in the present chapter.

It is against this backdrop that Sasaki describes Japan's fading wilderness. Land once trodden by wild animals has given way to walking paths for domesticated dogs. In recognition of human impact, Sasaki envisions Tarō moving between realms. Devoid of fixed identity, he may be read as progressive but is presented as a reinforcement of speciesist thinking. His subjectivity is as ambiguous as his body. A constant threat of disappearance is key to his persistence. This is why Sasaki refers to Komori as a "savior" (*inochi no onjin*). As such, he not only saves but also imparts life of his own volition.

Komori's instinct is to help Tarō attain his "species-specific norm of flourishing" (Nussbaum 2006, 365), trying his best to preserve as much of Tarō's canine self to earn his rightful place among humans. Komori wants to rehabilitate Tarō as a physical *and* social body. In this sense, Tarō is a prosthesis for Komori, who uses the dog to justify personal beliefs and transformations. Komori's rehabilitation of Tarō connects back to his own. As Nussbaum reminds us, such a process entails more than "blending in" by virtue of function: "For dogs . . . with rare exceptions, there is no option to flourish in an all-dog community; their community is always one that includes intimate human members, and so it is obvious that human support for their capabilities is morally permissible and in some cases required. Moral individualism says too little to guide us in such matters" (366). Recognizing dogs as a part of the human social landscape undermines the need for any serious awareness of their specificity in a human-centered context.

Limb for Limb

Owing partly to television coverage and Sasaki's well-received book, Tarō earned comparison to well-known memoirist and sports journalist Ototake Hirotada, who was born with tetra-amelia syndrome, a congenital disorder that rendered him essentially limbless. Ototake's autobiography was published in 1998 as *Gotai fumanzoku* and two years later in English as *No One's Perfect*. Upon giving birth to a child, Japanese parents may sometimes invoke the phrase *gotai manzoku* to convey the blessing of having a child with limbs intact. Ototake's use of the negative prefix *fu-* connotes a child devoid of them. This clever pun expresses his willingness to be self-deprecating in the face of this "deformity," which he sees as anything but, for it is all he has ever known.

Ototake's story shares much with those above. It has shades of Oscar in its blurring of corporeal borders. When, at age ten, Ototake's bones threaten to rupture his skin with new growth, he requires special surgery that mirrors Tarō's life-saving procedures. Moreover, a V-shaped scar left on his back by earlier treatments gives him a certain sense of pride. "Instead of being hard to bear," Ototake writes, "that scar began to seem more like a medal" (2000, 54). This admission finds an explicit parallel in Quill, whose defining birthmark also indicates a capacity for extraordinary things. That said, Ototake never wishes to feel "special" but a full participant in whatever is going on around him. His indefatigable spirit makes him very popular. Ototake never sees himself in terms of disability but includes it as a given in his self-imagining. The endearment of his book lies not in its boasting of personal accomplishments. Rather, he finds no greater joy than the optimism he instills in others.

Companion animals break down what Ototake calls "barriers of the heart," while those same animals are also exploited to reinforce them. For those unprepared to accept disability on human terms, animals offer a safety net. Ototake concedes the importance of conditioning when he says, "I always think that with the right environment, a person with physical handicaps like mine would not be disabled" (214), but he also knows such an environment is only possible when people are willing to give equal regard to all species and environments. The only true handicap is attitudinal, never physiological. This realization shifts disability beyond the model of inclusion into one of interrelation. Insistence on where one body begins and another ends, on what the body contains versus what it exchanges and shares, ceases to matter.

One consequence of *No One's Perfect* is that readers will undoubtedly interpret it as an affirmation. How inspiring, they might say, that he is able to overcome the obstacles of an "incomplete" body and live a "normal" life against all odds. And yet, the merit of disability is only inspiring when lived in pursuit of an ableist ideal. It is appropriate to say that "disabled" people are, like the boxes of normalcy into which others try to fit them, a fiction. One may assert knowledge of these imagined beings, whose "incompletion" renders them amenable to being filled in by overcompensations of sympathy while failing to see that dog and person can be connected by their apparent disabilities. If Ototake comes across as elusive for accomplishing day-to-day tasks with surprising ease, it is because he is portrayed as especially talented. But if it requires talent to hold and eat with a pair of chopsticks, why are nondisabled people not praised for it? Focusing on Ototake's ability to adapt to a lifelong condition disables *us*. In our astonishment over his basic survival skills, we forget that the most appropriate response might be unremarkable cohabitation.

People are just as likely to read about Ototake with animal interest as they are to read about Tarō with human interest. Ototake and (presumably) Tarō do not see themselves as disabled because their disability has always been their ability. His perseverance may look to the nondisabled like wild animality showing through the skin. It is as if, in the face of social constructions not typically built for disabled navigation, some primal urge is showing through the surface. This makes him more animal than human and contributes to people's marvel over his ability to be "one of us." Tarō, however, as a nonhuman, gets the "benefit" of seeming more human than human, willing as he is to overcome his disabilities when he does not even need to. In adapting to our ways, his humanity is praised above his animality as a quiet strength.

Because a disability like Ototake's is so visual, one can never ignore it as the basis for judgment and scrutiny. It boosts his actions to a level of perseverance that nondisabled people can only imagine. He will always be a wonder. He reminds us to keep our reactions in check, but in perceiving him that way, we never let go of his disabled status. In a manner of speaking, we are the ones who must train ourselves out of habits ingrained into our bodies from birth. This sort of muscle memory is difficult to shake and is where a different perseverance must take shape.

Tainted Commonalities

Peter Singer was among the key twentieth-century philosophers to widen considerations of sentience and morality to include nonhuman animals in his nuancing of binary debates around the topic of animal welfare. I join the feminist scholar Eunjung Kim in agreeing with Singer's (1990) foundational approach, as well as in her deviation from it on the point of passivity, which for her is central to corporeal imagination. Under terms of Singer's philosophy, disabilities bar certain people from their own humanity, which may be one reason disability scholars have avoided talking about animals. Yet Kim (2012, 104) would say that no autonomous agent is free from the controlling forces of passivity and that the conflation of passivity with worthless nonbeing is just as problematic as the conflation of agency with active being. So long as the possible spaces in which bodies may interact/retract, communicate/self-isolate, and injure/heal align with socially constructed limitations of normalized bodies, those bodies will continue to be their own boundary.

Rethinking what constitutes the body involves rethinking what it constitutes in turn. Bodies are predicated on an ideal of wholeness achieved through activity and functionality and in their promise of furthering the species. To destabilize the divide between subjects and nonsubjects is to doubt the integrity of subjecthood as the pinnacle of social mores. When a prosthesis—be it a wheelchair or guide dog—is nothing more than a passive receptacle for ableist desire, its vitality is unacceptable. Disabled bodies and their prostheses are not merely objectified but sworn to the "specific mode of intelligibility" (105) that confers upon them the status of objects. Kim's philosophy thereof revolves around a "passivity as agency" (95). As partners in a permeable and hybrid being, guide dogs and their users flow through each other in a mingling of embodiment and disembodiment that redefines humanness "so that it is based on the effort to fuse with objects, not on autonomous capabilities and sociability" (104). In one sense, the prosthesis promotes dominant expectations and stereotypes of disabled people. In another, it embodies disability's agentic powers to transcend the stranglehold of stereotypes. The human partner is as much a prosthesis to the guide dog as the reverse. This is one reason relationships between humans and guide dogs may seem strange or even perverse to those who would never entertain them. Few self-respecting people would consciously assume the identity of a prosthesis.

First and foremost, the above stories share an indefatigable belief in destiny. *Quill* takes this notion to eugenic heights through an overt interest in blood, breed, and hierarchical positioning. Gunji is similarly interested in Berna's breeding and purpose. As she writes toward the end of her recollection, "Berna, with whom I'd shared these past thirteen years, was a 'guide dog' from head to tail" (Gunji 2002, 297). Berna can only be identified by the duties for which she was bred and raised. A discussion of breed in the prologue of Tarō's biography likewise points out that purebreds should get the distinction of assisting disabled humans, while Tarō's genealogy is as covert as his disability is overt.

Disability undergoes constant reformation and, sometimes, decay. Hence a second commonality of these dogs: their fluid status. Quill goes from being the runt of his litter to beloved puppy to partner to orphan. Throughout, he maintains the stubborn demeanor of one determined to please. Berna goes from service dog to child to older sister to partner. Her transitions between stages are determined largely by an ability to integrate into her user's family life. And then there is Tarō, who is, in the most literal sense, a work in progress.

Status changes occur at key points in these texts, with Tarō raising the most difficult questions. Learning to cope with his infirmities to the point of ignoring them shows his will to live is as strong as a guide dog's will to assist. Between the two extremes of his transformation from discarded trash to vital agent exists a spectrum of purpose. Because so much of his inner development runs on a mechanism of self-preservation, Tarō turns the gift of life into agency. One gets the sense he is aware of all this, as evidenced by the determination with which he sets his mind to learning tasks inimical to his species norm.

A third commonality lies in human traumas. Growing up in the Niigata countryside, Gunji spent much of her childhood outdoors. While walking to kindergarten one day, a large dog came bounding out of the snow and pounced on her so suddenly that she almost fainted with fright. Though she was not hurt, "the fear I experienced then burned deep into my heart. That memory will never leave me" (14). When she loses her sight at age twenty-seven, the possibility of getting a guide dog is far from mind. She attributes her initial troubles in training with Berna to her hatred of dogs. To overcome this, Berna's trainer encourages Gunji to stick her hand into the dog's mouth. When Berna does not bite her, Gunji realizes she is kind and gentle. Only then does the training begin in earnest.

Komori harbors a deeper scar. As the child of a farming family, he observed his elders setting animal traps. One day, he got it into his head to set up a trap in the mountains behind his house, where he successfully snared a partridge. He snapped the bird's neck, as he had witnessed his father do on many occasions, but even as he proudly brought his catch home, he wondered why he had done so. Overcome by remorse for eating the bird at that night's dinner, he buried the remains and paid his respects. "But," the text goes on, "the taste left on his tongue was as indelible in his memory *as a stain*" (Sasaki 2007, 65, my emphasis). As with Quill's birthmark, the blemish of Komori's recollection represents empathy for the subhuman. Though described as a "rite of passage" (*tsūkagirei*) for any young boy brought up in the country, Komori holds on to this guilt for the rest of his life. Such experiences dissolve barriers between species. It is to the writers' credit that they should be included at all and that their errors should come across so productively.

A fourth and final commonality is the social ambassadorship that each of these dogs fulfills. In this capacity, Quill helps children briefly understand what it is like to be blind. Gunji, for her part, lectures about respecting guide dogs as working professionals who genuinely care about the safety of their users. Komori starts giving yearly elementary school lectures in 1998. His talk, entitled "Tarō and an Old Man's Dream," portrays Tarō not as a victim of disability but as one resigned to his fate. Komori leaves no doubt as to the moral thrust of his message. He openly laments the tragedy of youth suicides, attributing these not to teasing or childhood torment but to a deficiency of education, which sometimes fails to stress the importance of living. Tarō's sheer desire to live, he claims, shows that moral worth is hardwired into all living beings.

Komori's thinking on this matter piggybacks on a national agenda to promote life values. Anyone following the Japanese news during the summer of 2014 may remember the tragic case of a sixteen-year-old high school student who murdered and decapitated her fifteen-year-old classmate in Sasebo, Nagasaki prefecture. The murderer said she wanted to see for herself what it was like to kill and dismember someone ("*Hito o koroshite kaitai shite mitakatta*"), echoing the words of an Aichi boy who admitted to killing an old woman for the same reason ("*Hito o koroshite mitakatta*") in 2000. The girl also wanted to see inside a body ("*Karada no naka o mitakatta*"), betraying the morbidity with which one commonly imagines the transcending of physical barriers. The girl had been living alone in an apartment set up by her estranged father, who she once tried unsuccessfully to murder in his bed, and had "practiced" for the murder she ended up committing by killing a cat and putting it in the freezer, proving the accessibility of animals as intermediary sites of violence (Fujii 2014). In the wake of this incident, NHK news reported snap "welfare" sessions held in public schools by which students could be reminded of the value of life and the futility of taking another.

The relegation of discussion around outlying identities and social problems to classroom lectures, while not unique to Japan, implies a social ailment regarding the use of time, space, and energy devoted to messages of change. Animals can, and do, positively affect the ways children learn to understand their relationships with nature. In his Tarō lectures, Komori reminds audiences that schools are getting rid of class pets (typically rabbits), depriving children of the lessons they learn by caring for an animal. Tarō's lessons, he hopes, will go a long way in making up for that loss. In calling it "education for the heart" (Sasaki 2007, 100), he takes up Ototake's call to do away with barriers around the same vital organ.

Over outreach, I would suggest some form of "in-reach" as an effective way to learn about the possibilities between humans and companion animals. This process entails at least three lines of revision. First, it necessitates a fresher understanding of the relationship between blind persons and their guide dogs as one of hybrid rather than hierarchical design. Second, it invites a search for channels of continuity through shared traumas in a spirit of interspecies community. Third, it calls for an unscrambling of social programming around disability in recognition of the possibility that *everyone* is disabled in some way.

The Totality of Impairment

The above cases, with the exception of Ototake, deal with people or animals born "normal." Along this line of difference, I have charted a disparity of tolerances and engagements with their respective disabilities. Intriguingly, the more severe the disability, the more "acceptable" the subject. Tarō and Ototake expend relatively little effort to be welcomed by society at large. Amazement at their overcoming of even the most minor obstacles outweighs kneejerk discriminations. Nondisabled observers see Ototake as one possessed not of *dis*ability but of *hyper*ability, living in ways most would find frustrating.

Ōno Tomoya saliently corrects this dichotomy in his 1988 book *The Disabled, as of Now* (*Shōgaisha wa, ima*), in which he discusses Yoshimori Kozue and Shirai (then Tsuji) Noriko, victims of a birth defect epidemic resulting from thalidomide poisoning. Yoshimori and Shirai established a foundation called Cornerstone to conduct research on Japanese born with thalidomide-related defects. Of the 307 they interviewed, 60 percent answered "No" when asked, "Have you ever thought of yourself as a disabled person?" (Ōno 1988, 21). In a film version of her life (from which Ōno derived his book's title), called *Noriko, as of Now* (*Noriko wa, ima*), Tsuji Noriko says, "I've never known the feeling of having hands. It's never bothered me not having them, though I've sometimes wondered what it would be like" (21). Her body is "impaired" only when held up against the norm.

People with innate impairments are less likely to see them in those terms. "In other words," Ōno goes on, "a handicap is not a disability, but is rather an idea born of social entanglements with urban and industrial structures and people's own consciousness" (22). Similarly, impairments like blindness are better conceptualized as idiosyncrasies. Ōno sees disability as affecting everyone, disabled or not, and advocates "inclusion" (*fureai*) over "understanding" (*rikai*, 45). Yamashita Tsuneo (1984, 62–63) claims that the existence of an impairment as a matter of embodiment (*shintaisei*) is insufficient to explain discrimination against it and that it operates at a higher level of fear and detestation of disability itself.

Amid such rhetorical confusion, Wolfe offers a dose of clarity, reclaiming disability as a positive, "indeed *necessary* condition for a powerful experience . . . that crosses not only the lines of species difference, but also of the organic and inorganic, the biological and mechanical" (2008, 117, original emphasis). Wolfe's optimism bodes well for the future of transspecies awareness. Our conceptions of animals and people with disabilities "are forced to work within the purview of a liberal humanism . . . that is bound by a quite historically and ideologically specific set of coordinates that, because of that very boundedness, allow one to achieve certain pragmatic gains in the short run, but at the price of a radical foreshortening of a more ambitious and more profound ethical project: a new and more inclusive form of ethical pluralism that is our charge, now, to frame" (118). Despite the staying power of the narratives I have critiqued above, they promote messages of inclusion while obscuring the strategies for making that inclusion a reality. Because the distinction between behavior and treatment as sites of moral inquiry rides the line between passivity and agency, rather than the agency of disabled subjects (their triumphs, challenges, and advocacy), one effectively sees the *passivity* embodied by subjects across species lines, acting with neither the need for nor expectation of reward, recognition, and reciprocation. This leap of faith requires that one also consider what is to be constructed in place of human hubris by considering not the subject but what, in Wolfe's (2008) words, "comes after the subject."

We must think also of what comes *before* the subject to scrutinize the fields into which prejudices of subjectivity are sown. Doing this recognizes that respect between and for animals depends on the autonomy of both parties. Seeing the dogs profiled here as recipients of love is to deny their fundamental life. They must obey commands and respect their living spaces and companions just as their human counterparts. Love comes from the telling and retelling of their stories. It comes from the reportage of incidents, the management of expectations, and the endurance of emotional distances. To say all this is not to destroy their poignancy but to recognize that our role in training and loving them is rooted in the disavowal of objective authority. Disability is not something one "has." It is the intersection of competing social and physiological factors.

It is not clear to me how useful it is to say that our sympathy for Tarō is a form of humanization. It is a wish that we would all possess such perseverance beyond the things we do as givens. We may desire to be abnormal in the sense of doing something extraordinary. We may live vicariously through the successes of these animals, holding on to the belief that we would achieve these traits if only we could get in touch with something fundamental we have lost. Therefore, it is better parse the word "disability" in the following way. The prefix "dis" comes from the Latin meaning "apart" or "in a different direction," so rather than the separation of ability, it is the abling of separation. To be "abled" in the world means to go in a different direction from it, to assert one's individuality over the pervasive forces binding everyone and everything.

The wrench in the machine is that this process of attribution comes from a place of productive error. We see ourselves as bringing goodness to all animals by recognizing their potential for overcoming obstacles. But if this comes at the sacrifice of critical thinking, one must wonder who gains the most advantage: animals or the ones praising them? To praise animals in this manner makes "us" look as good as "them." By recognizing the social benefits of animals, we gain the same social benefits. This imparts all sorts of advantages when it comes to outlining, and putting into action, animal rights legislation. At first, the relationship seems equal. In accepting animals on their own terms, we resonate with what is in their best interest.

Herein exists the difference between reading an animal and reading *about* an animal. One collapses cognitive dissonances to the point of harmony between the two; the other engenders a general understanding and respect for, but not *with*, the animal. This is the area in which animal studies loses steam by ignoring the oppression of overcompensation. Extending extra sympathy toward the disabled of any species constitutes a hybrid act of courage and weakness. The schism between these two states is where one will find the stuff of error growing by cellular division. To choose one side or the other without acknowledging that schism is to be in denial of their integration and to misrecognize the stuff of this study as a reconciliation when, in truth, it is about seeking power over that which has power over us.

Whether or not Berna, Quill, and Tarō are just being dogs without conscious regard for the self, their transformations into death matter, as their essence is subjected to the productive errors of retrospection. Discussions of disability elide error as a mechanism for change, except to say its gaps must be filled by ideals of consummate function. To do away with barriers between species in life, I invite the reader to consider the antithesis. This will be the subject of the next chapter, in which I scrutinize the intricacies of disembodiment in the works of two major horror authors.

CHAPTER 3

Back to Life

"What we see as spectacle is in fact a ceremony."
—Louis Malle (cited in Kerekes and Slater 1995, 5)

These words from the French auteur Louis Malle point to what he called "sacred strategy," through the mediation of which, as a crafter of worlds, he entered a state of meditation or prayer. Thus, he implicated himself in every action and reaction on screen. As an agent of ceremony via the spectacle of terrifying events, horror authors are susceptible to the same characterization. The attraction of horror, which seeks control over that which threatens to control us, is the opposite of escapism for luring spectators into a guaranteed confrontation—one that, hopefully, they will overcome.

As burrs caught in the socks of our intellectual wanderings, animals cannot be pulled out without drawing blood. Animals in horror *must* enable trauma because they are its most convenient containers. When they confront their human counterparts, trauma resurfaces, expanded through detonations of hard truth. Horror literature in general, but especially that in which animals play a central role, depends on transfigurations. Rarely do these transfigurations lean toward divinity, pushing instead into corridors of the maleficent. Animals in horror are most often supernatural. The only way to deal with them is to excise them, a process that puts unimaginable physical and spiritual strain on those who must suffer at the edge of death if they are to escape with their lives, even if those lives are forever scarred by doing so.

Due to the boundary crossing of which they are so firmly capable, animals make harm explicit. They are double agents between good and evil, able to crush human naivety as easily as they can support it. To clarify this point, I have chosen two fictional stories that encapsulate the traumality of the human–pet relationship in ways that illuminate problematic nuances of ownership through productive error. The first is the short story "Flat Dog" (Heimen inu) by Otsuichi (the pen name of Adachi Hirotaka) about a girl, Yū, whose tattoo of a dog on her arm comes to life before mysteriously disappearing, forcing Yū to rethink her notions of body and border. The second is *Pet Sematary* by American horror icon Stephen King. Whereas Otsuichi primarily deals with *disappearance*, King deals with *reappearance* when protagonist Louis finds a way to bring the dead family cat back to life. Doing so makes him question his understanding of the afterlife and gives him a semblance of dominance in a domestic sphere where his authority has withered.

The parallax of "Flat Dog" and *Pet Sematary* yields an equation of self-awareness. Where Otsuichi navigates variables of personal responsibility, King denies access to that responsibility to begin with. Yū may be initially repelled by her tattooed dog's disappearance, but as her knowledge of their connection grows, so does her love for the dog, without whom she can no longer imagine life. The dog *is* her life, incarnate in all its fickle yet affirmative unpredictability. King's Louis travels in the opposite direction, falling from the grace of a loving family into a mockery thereof. Louis is anything but resigned to the hand dealt him and tries his utmost to jam the pieces of his misshapen puzzle into realignment. By the time he realizes the magnitude of his folly, he has dug himself into a pit with no rope.

Before cutting in, I offer a thumbnail sketch of horror as a genre in Japan and where King and others of his ilk fit into its streams of consciousness. As the reader will discover, King has a deep, if inadvertent, connection to horror in Japan, where his works have enjoyed wide appeal and influence. Animals in these two stories approach the same idea from opposite ends without ever meeting in the middle, where something more ineffable and frightening calls their authors into narrative service.

Animals in Japanese and American Horror

Japan has a centuries-long fascination with horror. Folktales and the Kabuki and Noh theater repertoires are replete with mysteries, illusions, and supernatural deceptions. Horror stories printed for mass consumption grew to prominence in the seventeenth and eighteenth centuries. Graphic novels during this time were especially popular and fell under the category of ghost stories (*kaidan*). Readers in the West will know some as the so-called *Kwaidan*, as collected by Lafcadio Hearn, but these constitute a fraction of tales compiled in the old capital, where "bizarre-but-true" tales and urban legends shared pages with long-established mythologies. At the same time *kaidan* were being devoured, animals were becoming a part of the literary landscape. Ghost stories about horses, monkeys, cats, otters, snakes, and (especially) foxes proliferated, and many would become immortalized on the theatrical stage.

It was not until Edogawa Rampo that mystery became intertwined with horror as such, as it also did through the fiction of his idol, Edgar Allan Poe, whose writing gained prominence during the Meiji and Taishō periods (1868–1926). By the 1920s, Poe had become a major influence on Japanese writers of that era, when aesthetic interest in the grotesque hitched a ride on Japan's catapult into modernism. Poe would also see a revival in the 1970s and 1980s when popular motifs from his fiction began to infiltrate Japanese visual culture through the media of manga and video games (Lippit 1999, 135). It should come as no surprise that the most popular of Poe's first stories to appear in Japanese—"The Black Cat" (translated in 1888 by Aeba Koson) and "The Raven" (translated in 1891 by Motoko Tadao)—revolved around animals. For readers used to taking animals as ciphers for human vices, Poe's characterizations were an easy sell during a time of great transition.

Animals have always played significant roles in Japanese mythology. In Buddhist parables, for example, every animal signifies one from a list of human traits: the fox's cunning, the fabled tanuki's mischief, the monkey's wisdom, and so on. Animals have carried over into contemporary horror, as related to me in an interview with occult author Asamatsu Ken. In Asamatsu's writing, prototypical in this regard, animals are no less symbolic. For him, they are the fury of nature incarnate. He borrows many mysterious creatures from Ainu folktales, which he then arranges idiosyncratically. But the one ruling over his dark menagerie is the dog.

Asamatsu's interest in dogs goes back to his childhood, when, in his words, a "truly ferocious" shepherd Ainu dog who lived next door "scared the hell" out of him. In his adulthood, Asamatsu has found a way to work through this painful memory by controlling it through the apparatus of literature. That he is so keenly aware of it means his use of dogs is *more* than symbolic, growling as it does in the darkest recesses of his lived experience.

Asamatsu reiterates the evil with which dogs have been associated. As servants of wickedness, they twist a loyalty more commonly associated with a positive human–animal bond into something of great menace. In the novel *Summoning the Black Hound* (*Maken shōkan*, hereafter, *Summoning*), he depicts the titular canine as a familiar invoked through a magician's cunning and influence. The entrance of the black hound in *Summoning* through incantation dramatizes the author's incorporation of a Western ceremonial rite of black magic into Japanese horror. Until that point, most horror writings, including his own, had drawn from domestic sources or motifs when it came to the supernatural. The black hound has since become a running theme in Asamatsu's fiction, particularly in the trilogy of which *Summoning* is the first installment. Asamatsu borrows his motif from tales of the British Isles, where the "black dog" once lurked in the fearful whispers of locals as a harbinger of death. "In addition to being a grand symbol for nature rising against conceit," he tells me, "it expresses the power of the *super*natural born of an occult technology." His reasons for choosing the dog are just as insightful. "At the end of World War II," he explains, "the Japanese military was eagerly devising ways to fight British and American forces using Shinto and Buddhist sorcery. Even as priests in Japan were putting deadly hexes on Roosevelt, the Nazis were researching the military potential of the occult. While working as a writer for an occult magazine, I heard tell of a Japan Self-Defense Force section studying these things, so I took this as a manifestation of violence for my series." The bond between black magic, animality, and the trauma of war is airtight.

In the West, animals in horror have likewise been symbolic, starting with Poe and continuing in the fiction of H. P. Lovecraft. Such animals are typically demonic, possessed, or otherwise altered by black magic or inexplicable forces. But nowhere has the pet become such an inescapable agent of horror as in the fiction of King, who became a major influence on Japanese authors when his novels began to be translated into Japanese in the late 1970s. Like his Japanese contemporaries, King situates animals squarely in the most fraught zone of modernity, which "finds animals lingering in the world *undead*" (Lippit 2000, 1, original emphasis). Their appearance is always something that *should not be* in a world that *can only be*, an impossibility made possible through suspension of disbelief.

Hidden in the Midden

Otsuichi, a young and prolific author of mostly short horror fiction, made his 1996 debut at age seventeen with *Summer, Fireworks, and My*

Corpse (*Natsu to hanabi to watashi no shitai*). Much like King, he presents fantastical elements as everyday facts, integrating them into the lives of ordinary people as catalysts for change. His characters deal with the consequences thereof by pursuing solutions to their most exhaustive, logical ends. Governed by no shortage of resourcefulness, they seek to undo what has been done to them, only to find that traces of disruption linger. They learn to cope through twisted resolutions, achieving closure in open wounds. Otsuichi's oeuvre is also entirely in the first person, breaking from Japan's "I-novel" (*shishōsetsu*) tradition in that his work, while confessional, is rarely autobiographical by its occlusions.

The Japanese title of Otsuichi's short story "Heimen inu" plays artfully with the theme of planes (*heimen*) throughout, the first and most literal sense of which comes out in the disorienting first sentence: "I'm raising a dog on my arm" (2003, 257). The "I" in this instance is Suzuki Yū, a high school student whose physical reality is disrupted by this cryptic discovery. The absurdity of possible scenarios in which this statement might hold true gives way to Yū's clinical explanation: "A blue-haired dog, about three centimeters in length. Name: Pocky. Male. Not what you'd call good looking, though the white flower in his mouth gives him a certain charm" (257). The dog is a tattoo, and his presence sets a most unusual tale in motion.

The second refraction of the titular "plane" appears in the circumstances under which Yū receives the tattoo. Yū's best friend, Yamada, dreams of becoming a tattoo artist like her father, who owns his own studio. One day, during an afternoon hangout session with Yamada at said studio, Yū is enchanted by a beautiful Chinese woman who is finishing her last day of her apprenticeship. The woman offers Yū a tattoo at no charge. Yū picks a photorealistic dog out of a magazine but ends up with the cartoonish one described at the tale's beginning. Despite her initial disappointment, she feels fate at work as planes of mindfulness and intention fracture and intermingle. Yū and the mysterious tattooist overlap like a Venn diagram showing slight affinity, even as their outer regions butterfly toward less definable infinities.

For the next few days, the tattoo itches intensely. Yū bears no grudge over getting the wrong tattoo. "I felt that the image and I had become one" (267), she says, and later admits to feeling "married" to the dog (279). Not only is she at one with Pocky, but she also senses the dog is alive. His smell becomes discernible, his barking wakes her up in the morning, and his pose changes in subtle ways—until the dog disappears from her arm altogether, reappearing on her midriff. The book in which this story appears is jacketed with that very image as if to show that

Pocky has a life of his own, but never apart from Yū's body. Yū suggestively exposes him in a way that privileges the viewer over even her closest family members.

Here is a third, paratextual plane. The cover art is a selective reveal, itself a manufactured skin "tattooed" with an emblematic image. It incites expectation ("Flat Dog" concludes this eponymous collection of four standalone stories), encouraging readers to wait until the end before understanding the image's haunting implications. One may already read aliveness into the artist's brushwork. Yū stands before a cloudy sky, dislocated in a liminal space where she seems unafraid of her canine sigil. Though her face is unknown to us, the dog looks up at her with contentment. A gentle confidence pervades the scene.

Back in the realm of her troubled tale, however, Yū hides the tattoo from all but Yamada. Amid this secrecy, she comes to face a gruesome reality as, one by one, everyone in her immediate family is diagnosed with some form of terminal cancer. At this point, Yū suspects Pocky has cursed her family with this round of death sentences. Yū's parents, meanwhile, are more worried about family finances. They harp on the likelihood of her being alone and unable to support herself in their absence. Forced to resign to this impending tragedy, she begins working at a convenience store in preparation for the slog ahead.

In addition to her parents' imminent death, Yū must deal with the immediacy of Pocky's life. Like any dog, Pocky eats to live, and Yamada is more than willing to help in this regard. By tattooing slabs of meat on Yū's arm, she accomplishes two tasks: Pocky gets his meals while Yamada gets the practice she needs—tattoo artists are best schooled on human skin—to improve her skills, turning Yū into a "human guinea pig" (293). At first, Pocky leaves tattooed bones on the skin, which eventually disappear. Much to her dismay, Yū never knows where Pocky hides them. The location of his midden is a mystery. This fact blurs the edges of self-understanding and turns her body into an alienated landscape. Yamada's solution to this discomfort is to tattoo boneless meat.

The increasing realism of Yamada's tattoos is a reduction of the body to its fleshy components and an indulgence of error as practical sustenance. By treating Yū's flesh as a canvas on which to inscribe images of more flesh, now severed and lifeless as food, Yamada turns Yū's corporeality inside out. It is as if the meat were being drawn out of Yū's flesh rather than being added to it in sacrificial offering to Pocky. As Yamada improves her artistic skills, she takes advantage of productive errors and shingles them into a platform for their shared commitment.

As it turns out, Pocky is a voracious eater—so much so that Yū sees him as a cipher governed solely by an instinct for consumption. He devours the white flower that once decorated him and even swallows a mole off Yū's face, along with another off her arm (foreshadowing a revelation mentioned later). Despite the makeover, she comes to see him as a dog with "no redeeming qualities" (299) and compares him to the archetypal Lassie, of whose cleverness, she wryly notes, Pocky possesses a hundredth. Hence my contention that error is not an ontological flaw but an opportunity for learning. "Without error," as Dominic Pettman (2011, 195) would have it, "we could not function, or rather, we would *merely* function." In this sense, Pocky comes seemingly preloaded with instincts that will never change, grow, or evolve. And yet, he foils those very developments in Yū and Yamada, who go along with Pocky's impossibility. He enables them to grow by being stuck in a perpetual, ageless state.

The tattoo is no metaphor for species but expresses its persistence in tandem with Yū's. Pocky's existence comes with great pains, both physical (in Yū's yield to the needle) and emotional (in Pocky's apparent connection to the family crisis), and proves to be far more invested in vitality than Yū first surmised. Pocky is even more alive for being a two-dimensional glyph. Because the eventual obliteration of Yū's entire family enacts a vanishing that parallels Pocky's, it would be unproductive to dismiss the dog as a receptacle for Yū's trauma. On the obverse, this interpretation recognizes that animals are aware of traumas (given Pocky's lifesaving qualities) while treating them as passive dumping grounds for our emotional trash.

Pocky shows his true colors when Yū accompanies her mother for a full day of tests. Yū wanders the hospital while she waits, buys a comic book from the gift shop, and sits reading it on the roof when Pocky begins to bark furiously, directing her attention to an elderly man who has fallen on the premises. Yū alerts the staff just in time to save his life. In response to the man's gratitude, she pulls up her sleeve to reveal the tattoo, saying, "It's *him* you should be thanking." The man stares wide-eyed as he is carried away on a stretcher (Otsuichi 2003, 300–301). Even as Yū reconsiders Pocky's determination as a sentient being, she decides that their relationship, such as it is, is too stressful for her to handle. After careful thought, she vows to transfer ownership of Pocky to someone else, her only option being to physically transplant the tattoo, skin and all, to another body. With Yamada's help, she finds an internet community of tattoo enthusiasts and posts a request for a recipient. There, she learns that the old man from the hospital, having neglected to ask Yū's name, has been searching for her since their fortuitous encounter.

This decision produces a unique problem of refraction as, sensing his time has come, Pocky vanishes, as much a part *from* her as *of* her. Desperate to rid herself of Pocky but unable to locate him, Yū asks Yamada to tattoo a "dummy" version of the dog on her left arm to convince the hospital administrator, who has agreed to arrange a meeting with her potential recipient. When this plan fails (the new tattoo is not quite the same), Yamada tattoos a leash and collar on Pocky when he reappears to keep him from running away. At last, they meet the old man, the president of a large company who values his longevity and of whom they know nothing more. Yū feels satisfied with his desire for the dog and believes, as does he, that it will prolong his life. But then, he asks Yū about her family. When she confesses her parents know nothing of the dog, the man shakes his head grimly:

> "It's just not right. A tattoo isn't something to take lightly. After all, your body is a sacred gift from your parents," he said like a teacher to his student.
>
> "Maybe you're right. Maybe I *did* get this body from my parents, and maybe it *is* sacred. But it's also my own. I know it was an impulsive decision, but I wouldn't take it back even if I could."
>
> "I'd never want to see you defile your body with such an image. I'm sure your parents would agree."

The old man continues down his moral track:

> "I'm sure it seemed 'cool' at the time, but I'm also willing to bet that, years from now, you'll regret it whenever you look down at your arm. Not that you'd know much about responsibility at your age, anyway."
>
> (325–26)

This last comment infuriates Yū, even as it makes her realize how much she adores Pocky. As she storms her way to the exit, she realizes she has been something of a Pocky all along to her parents, hiding when they needed her most. She resolves to be together with her family while there is still time to do so. She asks the receptionist for a box cutter and, in a sequence eerily recalling the finale of Michael Haneke's 2001 film *The Piano Teacher*, cuts a centimeter-long gash into her arm to free Pocky from his leash and leaves in triumph as the dog bounds happily around her bleeding arm.

This act of self-mutilation breeds a fourth iteration of inner (elemental) and outer (spiritual) planes. Yū's self-harm is her most productive error of all. In puncturing her own skin, she has broken the barrier between the interior and the exterior, between the truth of her animal core and her initial denial of it. Her separation anxiety eliminates any doubt over Pocky's function as a giver and a receiver of care, a fact underscored by a key disclosure: The moles eaten by Pocky were symptomatic of a skin cancer that would have killed Yū if left untreated. The dog has dealt her a royal flush against the bad genetic hands folded by the rest of her family, and the knowledge confirms her symbiosis with the dog in bittersweet terms. Yū has one more meeting with the Chinese woman, who touches up Yamada's dummy as a female, dubbed Oreo. In an epilogue, written as a letter of catharsis in anticipation of Japan's annual Obon festival, Yū discusses her life as an orphan and ends with a humorous postscript: "Only now I've got a serious problem on my left arm. These puppies never stop yapping!" (336).

It is worth noting that the Chinese tattooist, a mystical and exoticized figure, reveals a fifth plane. Not so much racially as she is geographically significant, she comes from a physical space far outside Yū's insular social sphere. The reader will remember that Yū's enchanting savior does not give her the dog she initially wanted. And yet, magic arises from that error. Otsuichi presents us with fuzzy lines of access by which Yū and Pocky become an entanglement of human and animal signatures. This is not to say they are one (this sentiment remains the projection of Yū's romantic idealism), but there is at least something of each in the other, a give and take of skin and sentience.

Pocky's navigation of Yū's bodily landscape amends the notion put forth by Stephen Laycock (1999, 274) that human understanding seeks knowledge through difference—in a word, through error—by stressing the urgency of self-alienation. The closer a species is in genetic or behavioral constitution, the more likely it is to mirror the human. And yet, for Otsuichi, the subjectivity of animate life is not ineffable but undecidable, which means that to treat it as *purely* one thing over another is to prevent the productive errors one might embrace. Pocky is anything but a reflection of the human, as confirmed by Yū's failure to dominate him. "Flat Dog" is a posthumanist tale insofar as it foregoes the animal as a moral prop in favor of acknowledging the animal as species-being unto itself. As a hybrid, "Yū-Pocky" defies the taxonomic reinscriptions of classical animal modeling in favor of stickier boundaries. "Flat Dog" turns the frightful conceit of error into an opportunity for self-understanding that no actual circumstance would allow.

The Three Cs

Watch any number of violent films, and you are likely to hear few complaints, beyond a general moaning over gratuitousness, regarding human victims. (The more gruesome and outlandish the death, the more likely it is to be admired.) But throw an animal into the mix, and suddenly, red flags go up. According to Baudrillard, seeing an animal treated as a human being in death repels us because we see ourselves in the animal: "In the hanged animal there is, by way of the sign and the ritual, a hanged man, but a man changed into a beast as if by black magic" (cited in Pettman 2011, 64). Is it simply that humans are animalized in death while animals are humanized? We saw some of this self-projection in the writings of Bandō Masako (see chapter 1), but there is more at play. Our willingness to accept the death of fictional humans stems from their having died for a reason. Because animals are not seen as individuals, they are taken to be universals. Writing, therefore, becomes synonymous with the death of the animal.

Death is neither an end nor a beginning. It is not a metaphor but a process that illuminates the porosity between animality and humanity. Death also undoes stalemated debates between individuality (particularism) and communality (universalism). With the page as his projection screen, Otsuichi demonstrates the chameleonic nature of one's engagement with mortality. Locations of and within, respectively, the particular and the universal are more prone to change within their social bubbles than without them. Death may be a process that connects all life, but it can never serve as a launching pad for liberation or egalitarianism amid disparate politics.

Any dog owner who has witnessed their pet go somewhere quiet to expire alone may be convinced dogs are far more in tune with death than we are. "Dog Whisperer" Cesar Millan confirms this hypothesis when he claims, "Human beings are the only animals who actively fear death, who actively dread death, obsess over it, and grieve over it—that is, *before* it happens. Dogs have so much to teach us in this area" (2006, 265). The many abused animals who accept their beatings as a fact of life, not to mention the dog who famously licked the hand of the man who vivisected him (Darwin 1876, 70), would seem to confirm this, yet one could just as easily interpret this surplus of compassion as a sign of thoughtlessness. "Dogs celebrate life, and they're okay with death," Millan concludes. "In fact, they are much better with death than we are. We need to look at them as our teachers in this department. Their natural wisdom can help us find comfort when we are facing our own human frailty and death" (Millan 2006, 264). Because we live so closely with these sages in disguise, their minds should not be closed to us.

This permeates what I like to call the Three Cs: containment, captivation, and capture. Each is a technology to be found in the apparatus of literature, which proceeds by process-oriented indeterminacies. As one theorist puts it, "Our pets are no longer wild. They are our captive audience and best students. Yet they have not lost their need to know us intimately. That knowledge has remained a matter of life and death to them" (Olmert 2009, 109). Through this acknowledgment of literature as capture, we might begin to dissolve the boundaries between "us" and "them." Through egomorphic projection, we see ourselves in the dying animal, *as* the dying animal. These are not moments to be feared but productively embraced.

Imagine the bullfight, among the more popular forms of entertainment in which the witting harm or killing of an animal draws a large crowd. In such fights, "the sense of conquest humans feel in the death, defeat, or dispiriting of the animal depends on the prospect that the animal can *feel* our victory and its own loss" (Fellenz 2007, 14, original emphasis). The bullfighter does not interact with the bull alone but with a multiplicity of sensorial cues and improvisations. Similarly, the pet "is precisely the place where those divergent senses link up and dissolve into one another, merging as well with the dusky odor ghosting around him like a cloud. Perception *is* this very comingling of different senses in the beings we perceive" (Abram 2010, 252–53, original emphasis). Akira Mizuta Lippit makes a kindred point when he says that "[b]ecause animal being is not thought of as singular, the death of each individual organism is survived by the entire species. All animals of a given species are, by this logic, extensions of one another" (2000, 172). Though indoor pets are welcomed into the family, the sheer volume of abandoned, abused, and neglected pets euthanized every year would seem to indicate that individualization of their deaths is not the norm. Rather, they are "added to the pile."

Pets have no temporality of life progression. Their death yields hindsight. The dead subject's life can be traced along any given arc. One cannot simply escape the obligations of life by giving up the ghost. In the words of Judith Butler (2004, 42), "perhaps there is some other way to live such that one becomes neither affectively dead nor mimetically violent, a way out of the circle of violence altogether. This possibility has to do with demanding a world in which bodily vulnerability is protected without therefore being eradicated and with insisting on the line that must be walked between the two." We might also see creative language as exactly that: something that creates rather than destroys. The literary death lends testimony to its evolving subjects.

In *The Prophet*, Kahlil Gibran philosophizes, "If you would know the secret of death you must seek it in the heart of life" (cited in Heinrich 2012, ix). Yet if no agreement can be reached as to what *constitutes* life—be it animal, human, or otherwise—then of what possible use are death's secrets? What if failings—death itself among them—are what expose those secrets for the taking? Such are the implicit concerns of Foucauldian biopolitics, which maps the methods by which living *and* dying are managed at the whim of sovereign power. Where biopolitics remains decidedly anthropocentric, posthumanism sees death as "the *in*human within us, which frees us into life" (Braidotti 2013, 134, my emphasis). Death enables life, is inextricably bonded with life, and negates the possibility of life by its absence or impossibility. Death is, in short, a "phenomenon of life" (Mulhall 2009, 101). Life thrives because it perishes.

Enter the "necropolitics" of Achille Mbembe (2008), who sees biopolitics as insufficient to explain the regulation of bodies, achieved not only through apparatuses of power but also through management of death and glorification of violence, sacrifice, and terror. The obstacle of biopolitics lies in Gibran's shortsighted idealism, for in it death "as a concept remains unitary and un-differentiated, while the repertoire of political thought around Life and bio-power proliferates and diversifies" (Braidotti 2013, 128). Even as fragmentation proliferates through necropolitics around memorialization and the veracity of its meaning, death functions as a constant, unchallenged in its power. The locus classicus of Freudian theory sees pleasure as a means of distracting oneself from the inevitability of death, as if, ultimately, the two were separate. For Heidegger, another prominent thinker on mortality, "animals . . . can only perish. Demise and dying are modalities of finitude to which animals simply do not have access" (Calarco 2008, 17; see also Mazis 2008, 33). And for Hegel, "the human being truly *becomes a subject*—that is, separated from the animal—in the struggle and the work through which he or she confronts death" (Mbembe 2008, 154). In light of such fatalisms, one's approach to death enables a certain mode of power made possible by life's passivity. Those subscribing to this view might say that any belief in animals as rational, self-aware beings endowed with souls is necessarily an atheist one, positing as it does the idea that "rationality does not prove immateriality" (Cheung 2010, 21), and would be one possible explanation for the distancing of pets in my corpus of interest. Posthumanism would spin it differently, seeing instead "the inter-*relation* human/animal as constitutive of the identity of *each*" (Braidotti 2013, 79, original emphases). There can be none without the other.

Death links humanity and animality and has the potential to undo their separation. It is not simply an act of posthumanism that seeks to enmesh these categories but also one of postmortality that equates death with nature, with the past and future of all things: "Death itself is more a transformation than a state; a dying organism becomes part of the wider life that surrounds it, as the hollowed-out trunk of a fallen tree feeds back into the broader metabolism of the forest" (Abram 2010, 269). Abram's cosmology here works death into something more porous and multidirectional than a theoretical event horizon: death as a rift, not an endpoint. It is, as Derrida might have put it, "an immanence *without* horizon" (Cavalieri 2009, 30). In the case of companionate species, death remains a looming inevitability and an activating force that opens as much as it closes. Our habit of interpreting any animal's death through understandings of our mortality is false, for death does not exist in us. Its consummation means the obliteration of rational thought and, by extension, ethics.

The hard-hitting emotional qualities with which human–pet relationships seem inherently endowed cast companionate species as subjects vulnerable to overwhelming desire. When Baudrillard (2001, 13) asks, "Why this fantasy of expelling the dark matter, making everything visible, making it real, and forcibly expressing what has no desire to be expressed, forcibly exhuming the only things which ensure the continuity of the Nothing and of the secret? Why are we so lethally tempted into transparency, identity and existence at all costs?" we might look to Otsuichi for one possible answer: because it gives us the illusion of control. Though one might attribute our fear of death to a stubborn willingness to forget it, that might just be another form of control.

Keeping Up Appearances

Where Otsuichi's "Flat Dog" deals with animal disappearance, Stephen King's *Pet Sematary* (1983) mines a primal pessimism. Though Otsuichi's disappearing dog frightens Yū at first, he proves to be a redemptive part of her. In King's novel, resurrected pets strip their owners of all possibility of redemption, leaving them addictively bonded to impossible new lives. Furthermore, whereas Otsuichi's dog is anomalous, the forces allowing resurrection to occur in King's fantasy are omnipresent. They are the spark of life in its darkest hour, pulled several rungs down the ladder of their autonomy to a state of morbid normalcy.

Like Otsuichi, King has always been an author fascinated with how ordinary people act in extraordinary situations and goes to extreme lengths to see how things will pan out for them. His characters show their truest selves in crises. Pets have played various roles throughout his later works—as alien hosts (*Dreamcatcher*, 2001), outlets for anger directed at humans (*Under the Dome*, 2009), and foment to a crumbling marriage ("L. T.'s Theory of Pets," a short story published in 1997)— but with nowhere near as much fortitude as *Cujo* (1981). This tale of a good dog gone bad is among his most chilling because the eponymous Saint Bernard is driven to kill not by demonic forces but by rabies. His rage, though seen as evil, is no more than the result of a disease born of nature's depths. Though Cujo tears his way through nearly everyone who stands in his way, we take comfort in the fact that those who have survived his wrath will never succumb to another attack. Not so in *Pet Sematary*.

Pet Sematary follows the demise of Louis Creed from a respected father and medical professional to a failure on both counts whose meek humanity primes him for the iron grip of malevolence. The Creeds are enjoying their new life in Ludlow, Maine, where Louis has been newly appointed as head of student health services at the nearby state university. Unresolved tensions of their move from Chicago linger, particularly in painful memories of Louis's trailing spouse Rachel. At first, their daughter Ellie, her infant brother Gage, and Church, the family cat, are impervious to the dislocation. When Church dies, and Louis finds a means to bring him back to life, the cat's return sets in motion a horrifying chain of events. The undead Church blurs distinctions not only between animate and inanimate but also between that which is animated and that which animates.

The second of those dichotomies undermines the validity of agency against a baseline of passive life. *Pet Sematary* strips humans—by way of animals—of their agency at the whim of a sentient evil with its own agenda. Willful death is the only escape from this evil and one's enslavement to it. The relationship between the animating and the animated in *Pet Sematary* straddles an equally fine line between embodiment and disembodiment. Reanimation imagines a miraculous realization of memory and points to a form of omniscience to which the novel's dramatis personae have no access. King's fixation on conviction-poor subjects relies on shadows wherein rules of natural law are broken to terrifying effect. I employ the word "animation" both as a rhetorical strategy to reconceptualize the threat of undead autonomy and as a literal function of the text.

King's undead invalidate arbitrary schisms between humans, animals, technologies, and environments. They preclude the possible existence of an animator by substituting the possibility of being *only* animated—in essence, imagining Pettman's errorless life. I read the "pet" of the novel's title not as a noun but as an adjective, describing less the ones buried in the cemetery and more the intensity with which the living covet the powers it obscures. King's cemetery is a physical space, a forest of makeshift tombstones and misspelled epitaphs left by children moving on from what are likely their first encounters with death. And yet, the cemetery, along with the life-restoring burying ground beyond it, is an object of adoration that gains power over all species. Any attempts on Louis's part to reconcile indiscretions in relation to raw animus leave him lost in the travesty of his search for solutions.

The absurdity of the *Pet Sematary* conceit—that a cat would return from the dead—becomes for Louis not a path to restoration of interpersonal harmony but a broadcasting of his lack of control. His bending of natural law, inasmuch as he understands it, throws into question what he believes about identity by ejecting it from an insular social hierarchy into a dialectical relationship with nature at large. He fears not that his cat has come back to life but that his cat has come back *without the need for life*, subsisting instead on the nutrients of a tainted soil. King's resurrections are as uncanny as they are wicked: the uncanny repels *and* attracts. Church 2.0 is alluring for his restoration, horrifying for the aura of wrongness that pervades it.

As Freud would have it, the horror of the uncanny (*umheimlich*) is its frontloading of repressed desires. "The source of the uncanny," writes Lis Møller (1991, 131), "is not the manifest element . . . but the latent—repressed or infantile—content this element leads back to." And yet, Møller would surely agree that Louis's resurrected cat possesses its *own* content. It is the double of a dead signifier, the uncanniness of which "pertains to the fact that the primary narcissism in which it originated has been surmounted" (132). Louis knows his actions go against the social norms into which he has been indoctrinated. His medical expertise assures the importance of maintaining those norms in his contributions to a healthy, ordered population. Still, he unwittingly abets a "narcissistic desire to reproduce life and thus to deny the power of death" (132), both an idealistic extension of his profession—doctors save lives, sometimes against odds—and a challenge to it. What unseats Louis is the return of that which he has habitually denied in himself.

Pet Sematary sidesteps ontological distinctions between living and nonliving bodies in ways that exempt animals from the subjective comforts of a privileged human species. Human–pet relations in the novel are firstly interactive and loving, secondly reactive and repulsive, and serve to prefigure parent–child relations, which are the spikes of the novel's electrocardiogram. King is willing to navigate the dankest corridors of reanimation by confronting Louis with animation in bare form, unsettlingly meshing pseudo-realistic bodies with autonomous function. In *Pet Sematary*, these anxieties find clearest expression and mediation through animals and children.

Though pets are an integral part of modern American life, *Pet Sematary* imagines what might happen if they could exist outside of that security, self-sustaining and, as it were, "off leash." By extension, King expresses interest in this same dynamic as it plays out between Louis and his children. By way of abreaction, Louis discovers the key to his family's precarious unity in Jud, a longstanding friendly citizen of Ludlow, who is more than happy to ease the newcomers into unfamiliar surroundings. Jud warns Louis of the heavily trafficked road that bisects their properties. "When a good animal gets run down in the road," he proselytizes, "a kid never forgets" (King 1984, 29). Prophetic words, these, in ways Louis will come to understand all too well. Before long, Jud brings the Creeds to the pet cemetery that lies at the edge of their property. Local children have maintained the cemetery for decades, and Louis is astonished by the time and care that have gone into its construction.

Jud describes Pet Sematary (so dubbed by those same children) in nostalgic terms, having once added to its number. Ellie, however, brings home from that place an interest in death she never entertained. Fearing the prospect of Church falling prey to that same fate, she quizzes her father on the mysteries of life. Louis tries his best to comfort his daughter when, after Jud's wife Norma suffers a fatal heart attack, Ellie asks Louis about Church. His fumbling answer prompts her to scream, "He's my cat! He's not God's cat. Let God have His own cat! Let God have all the damn cats He wants, and kill them all! Church is *mine!*" (51). Like Yū's relationship with Pocky, possession lies at the heart of Ellie's connection with Church and of her dawning awareness of the cat's, and her own, finite existence. Louis consoles her with half-baked secular wisdom, drawn at the intersection of his allegiance to science and his desire to placate a child's firing mind with images of an afterlife, hoping she will let the matter drop. A vivid desire to connect to Ellie's childhood innocence, to return to that state of naivety when he could not be held accountable for his failures, compels him to deflect the question.

His artful dodging of mortality fails him when Jud phones one cold morning with sad news: Church has been hit by a tanker truck and lies dead, a veritable popsicle, in his front yard. At this point, King clues us in on Louis's insecurities: "Church wasn't supposed to get killed because he was inside the magic circle of the family" (121). As luck would have it, Louis's family is visiting the in-laws (who detest him) for Thanksgiving when this tragedy strikes. Faced with unavoidable truth and out of a desire to help a man in whom he sees much of his younger self, Jud directs Louis to the Micmac burying ground some three miles beyond Pet Sematary. Louis buries Church in accordance with Jud's fervent instructions and returns home, unsure of what he has done or why he has done it. And just as he is prepared to break the news to Ellie, Church reappears, never the same again.

Church hisses when Louis comes near, acts erratically, and, in stark contrast to Pocky's disappearing acts, *appears* where he should not. Upon returning from Chicago, Ellie comments on his ever-present stench. What was once a warm companion in her bed is now a discomforting presence. Church is no longer the cat he once was. His resurrected form is trapped, as David Oakes (2000, 107) describes it, "between the no-longer and the not-yet." Jud admits to knowing full well the burying ground's power, claiming its pull is too visceral to resist once one knows it. The thrill of bringing back the dead never completely fades because one cannot ever disconnect oneself from it. He tells Louis of how he once used its powers to bring a beloved dog back to life, sharing both his concern for its lack of mind and fascination with its altered state. At any rate, Ellie ignores her intuition and accepts the deception, and life continues uninterrupted. That is, until an even greater tragedy strikes.

Gage dies. A few unsupervised moments during an afternoon play session are all it takes for the newly mobile boy to fall prey to another passing tanker. Louis's solution is inevitable, if only because any parent might do the same in his predicament. After the funeral, he sends Rachel and Ellie back to the in-laws on the pretense of recuperation. Jud, however, knows better and urges Louis to banish the possibility he is contemplating, assuring him that "sometimes dead is better" (King 1984, 166). Against Jud's protestations, Louis robs the boy's grave and reinters him in the burying ground. He waits for the inevitable, not knowing his actions are about to have drastic results. Back in Chicago, Ellie has nightmares of her father's deed, prompting Rachel into action. By the time she gets to Ludlow, however, Gage has murdered Jud and kills his mother in turn. Louis must then destroy his own son, and the cat, to staunch this chaos once and for all. And yet, because grief is the "battery that burying ground survives on" (395), he cannot resist bringing back Rachel, leaving an uncomfortable implication hanging in the air.

King may speak little of animality in *Pet Sematary*, but it is a central ligament pulling into flexion Louis's recourse to human reason and his relationship with his son. The immediacy of the undead body signals a shift in the logic of discovery to one of presentation. The blood flow of this logic pumps strongest throughout the burying ground and in the legendary Wendigo, said to haunt its spoilt earth. This mythical creature, a (dis)embodiment of cannibalism taboos among Algonquian peoples up the Atlantic coast into Canada, is responsible in the novel for cursing the burying ground, condemning any interred there to an existence bound by a hunger for human flesh (making up for the Wendigo's lack thereof). It is not the burying ground that activates Louis's considerations of reanimation but the Wendigo, who makes Jud and Louis outlets for his bidding. As Jud confirms, "The Micmac didn't discriminate, you know. They buried their pets right alongside their owners." This image sends Louis into a thought spiral, making him "think of the Egyptians, who had gone that one better: they had slaughtered the pets of royalty so that the souls of the pets might go along to whatever afterlife there might be with the souls of their masters" (135).

The Micmac may not have discriminated between humans and animals, but Louis has grown up in a society that does. His recourse to Jud's romantic notions of resurrected life makes him feel guilty for bringing suffering to the innocent animal—and, later, to the innocent child. Church's walking death provides an enigmatic resolution at best. Louis nevertheless treats it, as he describes it to Jud, as "something that was *meant*" (162, original emphasis). This echoes Yū's realization that she is bound to Pocky by fate. In both instances, the (re)animated pet refuses its status as an object of psychological manipulation, becoming instead something frighteningly real, primal, and shed of domestication. Louis and Yū use their pets for self-serving purposes.

The Wendigo, as an abominable species error, cannot be exclusively labeled as human or animal but flits somewhere, disconcertingly, between. As an interspecies blend that is taboo to a mind trained in modern Western medicine, the Wendigo is more than a figure to which Louis may anchor his compulsions. That the Wendigo is hidden from him until he sees its floating head as he transfers his dead son from the human cemetery to the burying ground again suggests that Louis does not deal well with appearances. While the Wendigo may be a powerful force, it gorges on weakness. Just as powerful is Jud's role as an enabler. On the one hand, he recognizes the dangers of resurrecting humans, having himself resisted the urge to bring his wife back from the dead. On the other hand, he lives out that dream vicariously through Louis. The burying ground exerts influence because it requires human intervention to transcend its perimeter.

The novel's mythological backbone supports the theological pressure of Church's name, which one might see as a warning not to tamper with God's domain. The tragedy surrounding Church is multivalent, involving at one level the fact of his death, at another the promise of a salvation in which Louis refuses to believe, and at a further level the fact that Louis can only become aware of that salvation by distancing himself from its grace through profane acts. He may earnestly expect his loved ones to live again, free from the sinfulness he so vehemently denies, but to do so, he must bow to the Wendigo, his counterfeit God. It is because of Church that Louis first considers letting Gage lie in his grave so that he and his family might start over again. But because Louis has already developed a taste for the Wendigo's power, he convinces himself that releasing Gage from his life would be tantamount to murder (299). He cannot bear, knowing that reanimation is possible, to be twice complicit in the boy's death. There is, however, a dramatic difference between the human child and the animal adult: Gage shows a glimmer of innocent self-awareness at the moment of his second death (402), while Church remains malevolent to the end. Gage's discorporate self somehow flickers into renewal, giving hope of an afterlife that makes his rekilling doubly tragic.

If anything about *Pet Sematary* makes it a horror novel, it is Louis's realization that he is a puppet of the same force that long ago compelled Jud to witness the soil's power. The Wendigo is an adept string puller. The possibility of something beyond human *and* animal posits a third, upsetting category that evades definition yet takes incontrovertible and fatal form in Louis's actions, which assume ritual logic insofar as they activate his fascination with the brute force of creation. Each of these figures—the cat, the boy, and the wife—stands like a trophy in the dimness of his uncertainties. As a set, they are vital because a) they make visible the traumatic errors of human injury that inform Louis's moral aptitudes and awareness of self-limitation, b) their displacement from the domestic sphere moves them beyond the scope of capture into the glare of irresolvable turmoil, and c) the more these subjects achieve autonomy, the more Louis loses his sense of humanity.

In a family where distance is an emotional staple, Louis expresses his inner life through the deaths of those he loves most. Despite attempts to rectify wrongs of which he becomes aware at the point of no return, the outcomes fall on powers he will never fully understand. He injects the living dead with his surrender—quite literally through the barbiturates with which he kills his son. King's insistence on the "evil" tendencies of reanimated beings is not the prescription of a sadistic literatus but the strategy of an astute one who, like Asamatsu, makes a crucial point: The servants of evil will always be expendable once they have fulfilled their purpose. Considering the uncanny circumstances under which the novel's relationships distort beyond easy parsing, one can no longer be sure where one role ends and the other begins. The resurrected Church may not have come to be without Jud's urging, but neither is the cat a slave to the man's will. He is the essence of his feline bearing, out of human reach. Through Church, Louis realizes the body is "at the mercy of psychological forces under imperfect control at best" (Innes 1998, 123). Gage and Rachel offer false promises of supreme control, while Church remains Jud's secret ante to the deal. Reanimation thrives on a commitment to "abstract emotional states" over "live emotions," the "generalized or generic, rather than individual terms" of their nature (123). Louis's cat and son, once-subjective beings culled from a stable reality, transcend that very reality, "holding the mirror down to nature," to borrow Edward Gordon Craig's phrasing (cited in Innes 1998, 183), reflecting what Louis refuses to see: that death is nature personified.

Of all the frights King has purveyed, *Pet Sematary* disturbed him to the point where he found it difficult to finish. As he writes in an introduction to the 2002 Pocket Books edition, "*Pet Sematary* is the one I put away in a drawer, thinking I had finally gone too far. [. . .] Put simply, I was horrified by what I had written, and the conclusions I'd drawn" (2002, xi). What is especially frightening about *Pet Sematary* is that there is nothing extraordinary about it. It is, in a sense, "intraordinary." The novel's undead are animus incarnate, and Louis seeks control over them because, through them, he can only pantomime self-control. It is a deceptive vision that blinds Louis to death encroaching on his dwindling worldview. This does not mean any understandings of autonomy are doomed to morbid ends but that the objects we infuse with those understandings may outlast us.

Vanishing as Belonging

To deepen our understanding of these deaths and to connect King's tale to aspects of modern Japanese life, I look to *Bones of Contention*, in which author Barbara Ambros spatially and temporally examines the "necrogeography" of pet memorial rituals. Japan's relationships with animals are far from culturally unique, given their connections with pre-Buddhist Chinese philosophy, religious cosmologies that can be traced to the Indian subcontinent, and neo-Confucian thought, in addition to questions of geographic location, historical situatedness, and social class within Japan itself. Neither have animals, even in Buddhist terms, always been seen as "beastly" and uncouth. In parables and other didactic writings of the Heian period, "animals sometimes served as moral barometers that could reward or punish humans." Ambros significantly goes on to write that "beasts were often shown to be unfailingly grateful: they usually repay human kindness and compassion with acts of sacrifice or the granting of wishes" (2012, 37–38).

Ambros also sees pet memorial rites as "a response to modernity with its inherent commodification and consumption of animals" rather than as emblems of longstanding tradition or reverence for nature (10). Connections to military action and industrial operations such as whaling also contributed to reinforcing those industries through notions of sacrifice. During the Tokugawa period, for instance, a time famously put under the microscope for the advent of Tokugawa Tsunayoshi's "Laws of Compassion," Buddhism was very much on people's minds. When whaling rose to prominence as a topic of scrutiny, the hypocrisy of making a living by killing was far from lost on the public. Notes Jakobina Arch (2018, 151), "The deaths of whales, out of all possible animal deaths, were commemorated in the most human fashion, with posthumous Buddhist names recorded in a death register." This allowed them to be prayed for as their souls continued in the reincarnation cycle. "Domestic animals," she adds, "generally did not get this same treatment, and the few early memorials for horses, dogs, or cats did not appear until nearly a century after the construction of the first whale memorial" (151). As industry and activity boomed in the modern era, so did an underlying tension regarding humanity's desecration of animal life, leading to an increase in animal rituals for the soul's appeasement.

Considering this moral struggle, Ambros (2012) refutes the linear and reductive perception of Japanese living in harmony with nature being forcefully ejected into modernism. Instead, she observes a more realistic blend of sacred and utilitarian purposes in those relationships than the forced harmonic structure of the collective psyche. Such ideas have been reinforced from within and without Japan. No such harmony has ever been the norm, or even necessarily the baseline, of ethnic Japaneseness. Japan has always straddled the line between an aesthetic love for nature (as seen in its creation myths and medieval court poetry) and a humanistic subversion thereof. All the while, ritual has acted (in both the agentic and theatrical senses of the verb) as an important space of mediation between these two worldviews.

Currently, pet owners in Japan tend to use the term "my child" (*uchi no ko*) to refer to a pet. Seeing an opportunity to gain income in a changing society, temples began to think more seriously about memorializing these new family members. Ambros links this trend to an extensive chain of events: "Urbanization, the increase in single and nuclear-family households, delays of marriage among both males and females, the falling birthrate and graying of society, the occult boom of the 1980s and early 1990s, the pet boom of the 1990s, the antireligious backlash in the wake of the 1995 Aum Shinrikyō incident, and the spread of pet loss counseling and the Internet in the late 1990s have been contributing factors that led to the particular constellation of practices in contemporary Japan." Thus, the "hybrid status of pet memorial rites" is confirmed and makes them more than worthy of scholarly inquiry (7–8).

In contrast to the publicity of human funerals, which may include "not only the nuclear family but also friends and coworkers, pet funerals are usually limited to the nuclear family" (9–10). This necrogeography of Japan shows us how pets, despite being welcomed with increasing acceptance as family members, more often run aground once they enter a state of death, which reinforces species hierarchies and other status markers among the living. The effect is such that despite having the appearance of humanness, postmortem rites for pets operate within spaces that separate those pets from their owners. For instance, even when the idea of jointly enshrining pets among dead ancestors on Buddhist altars came into wider prominence in the first decade of the twenty-first century, the agreement among ritualists was that pets were subordinate to human ancestors, themselves orthodoxically subordinate to the Buddha. Cemeteries, too, are places of inclusion and exclusion, welcoming the dead while elevating human remains above those of animals, which are legally "waste."

Throughout her fieldwork, Ambros witnessed a range of reactions and methods of mourning. At pet cemeteries, she "often observed that pet owners treated the urn with the cremains of their pet as if the pet were still alive: cradling the pet's urn in their arms as well as gently petting or stroking the urn as if they were touching a live animal" (141). Moreover, she shares a poignant account of an elderly woman offering incense to her dead pet in place of a memorial tablet or photograph. Invisible yet still the focus of worship, the pet is a personal talisman connecting the realms of the living and the dead (138). Both ways of communing with the dead embody shades of traumality in their reliance on mediating objects—whether physical or immaterial—to assuage them.

In like-minded research conducted in cat cafés in Japan, Lorraine Plourde sees cats as central animal mascots of Japan's "healing boom" of the early 1990s. As spaces of affective labor, these cafés delineate cats as objects on the one hand and laborers on the other: "It is precisely the unruliness and flexibility of the cats that is instrumental to the café's production of a feeling of domesticity and home" (2014, 3). Some such venues go to great lengths to tout their cats as distinct individuals (one café, for instance, has given its star feline a Twitter account). Plourde sees this as "an intriguing example of the increasing immaterialization of the economy in post-industrial Japan" (18) to which pets are easily adapted.

These new materialisms focus on processes over forms (Coole and Frost 2010). They inherently criticize the broadening of ethical landscapes to include "bio"-prefixed notions (e.g., biopower, biopolitics, biosphere) and see two possible directions in this move: a deference to the invisible forces that shape us and a desire to dominate those forces. New materialists see a particular *biopolitical anthropomorphism* at work, by which they mean "the biopolitical processes that bring about the centrality of the human and of certain humans; and the tendency of biopolitical analyses to reinscribe this centrality by taking human species as the primary basis upon which cleavages of race and sex occur" (Livingston and Puar 2011, 8). One only gets used to things animate and inanimate when they are incorporated into material life. The death of the pet-object invites a pause over the actual "materialism of the encounter" (Coole and Frost 2010, 35, citing Althusser) whereby the randomness of things becomes its own web of materiality. In the words of Haraway (cited in Giffney and Hird 2008, 5), "Theory is *anything* but disembodied." It is written on the body. It *is* the body.

As pets are an increasingly recognized (and recognizable) part of what Ambros terms the "necral landscape," even if their remains are still being "relegated to marginal spaces on the Buddhist altar and in the cemetery" (2012, 155), they take on deeper valences in death than in life. "We live cut off from the universal chain of life in an age when our absolute trust has no object," says Ōmura (2009, 141), pointing his analytical telescope into this issue's galactic center. Without a focal point for trust in life, latching on to the least likely symbols in death becomes the next best thing.

Thanks to medical and dietary advances, parents rarely outlive their children anymore. Therefore, "because we no longer have to experience the death of a child, separation from a pet is the only opportunity for us to grasp the *ephemeralness* of life" (146, original emphasis). Whereas cremated humans are said to be "returning to everlasting nature," the spirit of a pet clings somehow to its remains. Most major religions "disavow the idea that consciousness binds the soul to a place of mortal rest" (148), while neo-animism holds that the souls of the dead never leave their places of burial. As Ōmura notes further, "it's not that pets are treated more like humans, but that the death of people is being treated more like that of pets, and this reminds us of that" (49–50). One might think the borders between pet and owner would be more permeable, but this phenomenon only seems to reinforce them.

More people than ever in Japan are having prayers intoned in perpetuity for their pets, a practice historically reserved for children whose lives ended prematurely. Ōmura takes this to mean that ancient peoples resigned to the possibility of watching their children die possessed "sensitivity toward human relations and of their fleeting nature" and "became aware of this unconsciously through petkeeping" (152). Was this the origin of neo-familism that recognized the fleetingness of life as opening people to love?

Ambros rightfully argues that "[t]he inherent tensions between views of animals as fellow living, potentially divine beings and of animals as lower beings that ought to serve human purposes are resolved through ritual," which partly explains the prevalence of pet funerals (2012, 9–10). These often-private affairs act as leveling mechanisms—mediations that, in being so codified in the rigid observance of death, serve to alleviate remaining tensions. Were human–pet relationships *not* fraught with such tensions, these rituals would serve very little purpose. The pet dies so that it may live on.

How apropos that "error" becomes "terror" with the addition of a single letter. Otsuichi and King have much to say about the morbidity of error: its penchant for rupture, open wounds, and self-mutilation. Then again, one engages with writers like Otsuichi and King for their affirmation of life. In reading about and imagining their horrors, one becomes accustomed to their rhythms and learns to change their minor keys to majors through transpositions of hope. After becoming aware of Yū's coming of selfless age or Louis's deadly cycle of playing God, one can only marvel at the fragile purchase of our identities.

The concept of vanishing appears centrally in the work of John Berger (1980) and Lippit (2000). Berger sees animals as subjects in a state of perpetual vanishing. Lippit strengthens this interpretation by calling animals, at one point, "spectral" (1), at another, "cryptological artifacts" (189). Such approaches underappreciate the fact that perpetual vanishing is only possible when animals exist in a state of perpetual (re)production. It is not that the methods by which animals appear have been curtailed but that the sheer scale of their proliferation disallows us from processing them all at once. The imbrication of appearance and disappearance is necessary to live in linear time. Otsuichi and King are constantly killing and reviving animals as collateral damages of modernity but also as indivisible foundations of it.

For a philosophical, if circular, account of vanishing, we may turn to Martin Heidegger, whose unpacking of Friedrich Hölderlin's "Stimme des Volks" (Voice of the People, circa 1800) provides relevant instruction. Heidegger zooms in on the poem's first two strophes, translated as follows by William McNeill and Julia Davis:

> Unconcerned with our wisdom
> The rivers still rush on, and yet
>
> Who loves them not? And always do they move
> My heart, when afar I hear them vanishing
> Full of intimation, hastening along not
> My path, yet more surely seaward
>
> (1996, 27–28)

The poet describes rivers as "vanishing" and "full of intimation." Their movement is constant and flows without the need for human touch.

"They are thus remote and foreign to humans," says Heidegger (28) of their rushing spirit. And yet people rely on rivers for sustenance, travel, and habitation. Animals drink from the same waters, self-determined and lacking the need for humans yet necessary to us as sources of food, transport, and labor. In addition, we rely on animals for fashion, beauty, creativity, and, above all, language (they were, after all, visual building blocks of the earliest writing systems).

Humans may follow animals and nature, but Hölderlin's rivers do not follow humans. Rather, "The rivers' intimative vanishing along their own path is like an abandonment of the realm of the human landscape" (28). This balance of intimation and vanishing marks Otsuichi's story, in which the dog's penchant for concealment and the strategy of his becoming speak to a "both-and-neither" scenario. The intimation comes in Yū's growing attachment to her tattoo and to the lives it destroys and saves. Pocky is at once a remnant of the past and a cornerstone of the future. As Heidegger likewise notes, "the vanishing of those who vanish is not simply a crude vanishing into whatever is finished and bygone. Vanishing can also be an inconspicuous passing away into what is coming, into a decisive belonging to whatever is coming" (29–30). Pocky's playful disappearances entrench his connections with the yet to be, giving Yū the full brunt of his phenomenological being.

Heidegger delineates another helpful frame. Looking at two complementary versions of Hölderlin's poem, he concludes that "the essence of poetry is joined to the laws which strive to separate and unite the hints of the gods and the voice of the people. The poet himself stands between them. He is the one who has been cast out—out into that *between*, between gods and men. But first and only in this between is it decided who man is and where his existence is settled" (Heidegger 2000, 64). One might see literature, too, boxing the animal as an agent of human interest and an intermediary to a great unknown. The human may stand at a crossroads, destabilized by the illusory universality of language, as intimated in Otsuichi's obsession with Pocky's errorful wandering into Yū's lesser knowns. Yū's reaction to Pocky's disappearances is silence. She has no words for her body and requires the privilege of retrospection to make sense of this unbelievable episode in her life.

Mechanisms of vanishing impute the construction of language, which alienates the subject as part of a universal order. If anything, it *requires* alienation for universal membership. What sounds like a paradox in theory unifies through practice. In Hegelian terms, narrative acts feed illusions of universal belonging into which the subject effectively vanishes, nameless and secure in the knowledge of self-preservation. In one scholar's estimation, "[t]his movement of self-preservation through others is the movement of universalization through perception. Death initiates this movement of preservation through annihilation. Language emerges seemingly out of nowhere. The mysterious relation between language and death is contained by this paradox of perseverance through disappearance" (Oberst 2009, 120). The failure of language to communicate the ineffable animal is also its most colonial aspect, making the division of time and space appear for all intents and purposes natural, beyond human, and belonging to an incomprehensible afterlife. Only through language can humans constitute indivisible being.

All of this points back to Otsuichi's story, the vanishing point of which has been shifted offscreen. It now exists somewhere within Yū and comes to define her in relation to what she cannot see. Pocky's trickery denies Yū as a viewing subject while wholly embracing her as a part of his totality, just as he is now a part of hers. Self-directing yet molded by Yū's maturation, Pocky is her conceptual focal point. He serves to animate and define those things reaching toward, and issuing from, her body. The vanishing subject has become its own pet. It takes on a theory of vanishing as a mantra, finding strength through repetition and intimation. Yū's self is an affordance of becoming, which plots its being in a continual redrawing of coordinates. Where vanishing—in the sense that Berger and Lippit scrutinize it—is for animals a form of captivity, for Heidegger, it serves as a trigger of intellectual freedom in the human subject (Tran 2011, 106). This is where the "magic" of literature begins to undo the laces of the Anthropocene.

Heidegger disinters one further clue in the similarity of his interpretation of the river to animal life. "It is precisely that which tears onward more surely in the rivers' own path," he writes, "that tears human beings out of the habitual midst of their lives, so that they may be in a center outside of themselves, that is, be ex-centric." He goes on: "The sphere proper to standing in the ex-centric middle of life is death" (1996, 28). This recurring theme of death throws light on the arbitrary schisms between humans and animals and supports the delineations of Otsuichi and King, both of whom break up the path of mortality—which should be a one-way street—and repave it as a two-way thoroughfare.

With that in mind, I move on to my final chapter, offering the strangely optimistic *Mr. Turtle*, an astonishing piece of science fiction by Kitano Yūsaku, as an example of the destructive and healing properties of the cyborg. In actualizing a dual purpose, the novel's artificially intelligent protagonist treats death as a new beginning, a catalyst for constructive thought and building of world-self. In this regard, Kitano has written an anthem for the future of human–animal relations.

CHAPTER 4

Shell Is Other People

"Because it requires flights of speculation, as well as because it requires collaboration among many separate entities, science can never be purely human, nor purely rational."

—Steven Shaviro (2016, 13)

Bruce Shaw's *The Animal Fable in Science Fiction and Fantasy* was innovative for homing in on the role of animal mythologies in science fiction (SF) through a survey of its subgenres. Van Ikin begins his foreword to that book with an intriguing claim: "Animals are aliens, of a kind" (in Shaw 2010, 1). In the book's conclusion, Shaw concurs: "Are we alone in the universe? No, because there are animals who share our lives with us and stimulate our imagination, as I am sure we do for them" (222). Tongue-in-cheek though it may be to view animals as aliens among us, the practical value of this framing is dubious. While Shaw tries to put humans and animals on an even keel, animals remain subordinate, peripheral to a human center.

Whether surpassing their human enablers like the genetically modified dolphins of David Brin's "Uplift" cycle (1980–98) or seeking to destroy humanity in a quest for global domination like the hormonally triggered animal warriors of Robert Repino's 2015 *Mort(e)*, animals in SF tend to be enslaved or devalued subjects desirous of power. And whenever humans encounter legitimate, nominal alien life forms in SF, these entities often assume reptilian, crustacean, and feline traits. The effect of this tendency is twofold, distinguishing aliens from terrestrial humans by building off the otherness of animals on Earth while hollowing out conduits for reader sympathies. As misunderstood subjects, animals map well onto alien species whose inner lives may be just as vast and mysterious as the light-years of traversal required to reach them.

A sizable portion of English-language SF's animal-themed classics, in addition to having been written by women (e.g., C. J. Cherryh's "Chanur" saga), assumes a feminist slant. Margaret St. Clair's eco-political *The Dolphins of Altair* (1967) and Carol Emshwiller's witty allegory *Carmen Dog* (1988) degauss the boundaries of gendered subjects in earthly crises in the face of which entire social orders stand on the brink of destruction. The go-to solution for fallout is a dramatic reshuffling of failed hierarchies in which animals become convenient placeholders of uncertain futures even as humans struggle with the present. Despite these salient identity politics, few authors ever dedicate space to examine their own animal appropriations.

Aware of this hypocrisy far ahead of the game, Donna Haraway (1994) offered her influential "A Manifesto for Cyborgs," therein taking creationism, and even strands of mainstream feminism, to task for leaning too heavily on allegorical formations without addressing true, boundary-crossing relations with animals and technologies through which the centrality of the self might be undone. Yet even as she sought to loosen categorical restrictions, Haraway outed the cyborg as a tool of masculinist warfare. In this respect, she defined the cyborgian reality as a domestic one—which is to say, as a mental construct that must confess its physiological ties to a patriarchal nervous system if it is ever to fashion a body politic of its own.

SF rarely denies the fixity of the animal as a category because the genre has yet to reconcile the fluidity of the human. Animals remain anchor points in which authors might find traction in an otherwise slippery landscape. Far too often, animals are little more than stand-ins for their human counterparts, of whom they function as "universal" signifiers. Even Olaf Stapledon's *Sirius* (1944), one of the most plausible extroversions of the canine in all of fiction, is a thinly veiled commentary on World War I. As a laboriously detailed character study, Stapledon's tragedy of a cerebrally enhanced dog who loves a human woman shares too many parallels with the author's biography to be seen as more than allegorical fantasy. Such alterity is more than a result of the "cognitive estrangement" so famously attributed to SF by Darko Suvin (1979, 3). It is a gaping black hole that obscures animals' posthumanist potential.

It is impossible to summarize SF without acknowledging the vital roles animals have played within it. On the one hand, their ubiquity allows readers to recognize the limitations of our imaginations. On the other, SF reinforces the otherness of animals by treating them as backyard enigmas. But if the only unifying factor of the genre is its humanity, then how can it possibly alter relations between species? To answer this, one need only point to the vast philosophical developments of SF and its proliferation of expansions, divisions, and hybridizations alike as an "evolving mode" (Seed 2011, 2) of life itself.

And then, we have Kame-kun. The eponymous protagonist of Kitano Yūsaku's 2001 award-winning novel, published in English in 2016 as *Mr. Turtle*, redraws the parameters and phenomenology of artificial intelligence (AI) around questions of animality and designer consciousness. Kame-kun's nonhuman appearance and nonallegorical temperament separate him from other "animals." The conceptual framework of *Mr. Turtle* and its author's approach to enmeshments of humanity and animality present a compelling possibility for, and cautionary tale of, the trajectory of human–animal relations.

Kitano revels in the semantic potential of his species of choice, evidenced by the neologisms that pepper the novel and constitute a story unto themselves. The first part, entitled "Replican[t]urtle" (*repurikame*), epitomizes Kame-kun's hybrid physicality. The portmanteau fully and concisely expresses his semi-constructed life. The second part takes the title "Robo-Turtle" (*mekame*), underscoring Kame-kun's functionality as a machine. The third part, "Turtle Recall" (*kamemorii*), picks the scab of a violent backstory. Finally, "Turt[le]tters" (*kameeru*) signals Kame-kun's penchant for writing and electronic communication. By introducing these terms, Kitano engages the power of naming to suit a future in which humans and animals may not only coexist but also co-consist. As Akira Mizuta Lippit (2000, 161) observes, "The changes to language that the figure of the animal effects also open another realm for animals to occupy." Each term is a window into Kame-kun's phenomenological world. As a machine produced by and for humans yet modeled after his turtle counterparts, Kame-kun takes on characteristics of both. Each of these species worlds is a mirror of the other, the infinity of reflections between them serving as a playground for Kitano's authorial tumbling. Through his rudimentary understanding of creation, Kame-kun forges a personal philosophy of bodymind in relation to space as his world morphs into a self-magnifying spiral into which the reader becomes pulled by association.

Because science fiction is an embodied literature, Kame-kun's life feels much like our own. Its surface is pockmarked with jacks into which we might graft any number of compatible wires of understanding.

Kame-kun is more than a machine. He is what Bruno Latour (2005) calls an "actant," an active agent suffused with goal-oriented purpose. Kame-kun is his own actant but is also part of a network of others whose weblike communication can be switched on at any moment. While he is a "replican[t]urtle," he is an individual guided by a question that is uniquely his.

Such dynamics are familiar to the Kitano fan, who will have encountered a variety of animal subjects in 1994's "Adrift in the Jellyfish Sea" (Kurage no umi ni ukabu fune), 2001's "Crayfish Man" (Zarigani man), 2002's "Planet of the Squid" (Ika seijin), 2011's "Fox Possession" (Kitsune no tsuki), and his six-part series of animal picture books for children, published in 2003. Enlivening these works is a special interest in respective animal worlds, clarifying a need for disembodiment in a future of compromised borders. As Istvan Csicsery-Ronay has it, such technologically minded utopianism "has obviated the need to use animals as willing slaves, a function that they may no longer need to serve, given the arrival of machines. Their continued existence benefits human science now rather as texts to be read and rewritten" (2008, 253). In this sense, the specificity of Kame-kun lies in his AI. Though, at its most ideal level, AI promises autonomous and victimless technology, it is a seamless means of justifying enslavement. Kame-kun confirms the textual metaphor with idiosyncratic honesty. His status as a biomechanoid christens the vessel of his animality with a bottle marked INDIVIDUALITY, even as it docks him as a human creation. Connecting these arbitrary opposites is his shell, which functions as the novel's boundary par excellence. If anything unites SF under one motivic umbrella, it is space—both outer and inner—and the ways in which it affects tendencies of inter-technological—and, in this instance, interspecies—relations.

Introducing Kame-kun

Mr. Turtle tells of a cyborg turtle of the same name assaulted by horrific, if vague, memories of fighting in a war on Jupiter, after which his memory was wiped and he was integrated into human society in anticipation of the next interplanetary conflict. In the interim, Kame-kun lives among humans, doing human things. He works a blue-collar factory job, rents an apartment, and enjoys going to the library, where he even makes a human friend. But he is constantly wondering about life and takes long walks to ponder the mysteries of his place in the grander scheme of things. All the while, he must deal with constant discrimination from a society that treats him as a reminder of a war no one wants to think about. His life continues in this way until he is found by his manufacturer, who prepares him for another reset before going back to Jupiter.

Though Kame-kun will be recycled into the symphony of war, his instrument—his self-questioning AI—proves that even matter deemed inanimate except by human intervention must express its will to power. Kame-kun's interest in life/afterlife, love/hate, and materiality/immateriality comes from a consciousness that grows as he grows. What appears to be a youth-oriented fable of a turtle fending for himself in a human world turns into a treatise on the purpose of intelligent life. Questions raised by *Mr. Turtle* are thought-provoking, softening human–animal barriers in ways rarely seen in even the most speculative literature. Though SF is not necessarily the only realm in which techno-species assemblages may flourish to this extent, Kitano's insight accepts the voice of his cherished assembly with an open ear.

Said assembly comes in the form of an army of cyborg turtles, Kame-kun among them, once sent to Jupiter to battle a legion of giant crayfish. The latter are the result of a massive human error when a film production company created them as biomechanical "dummy" victims of realistic onscreen killings for *kaiju* blockbusters. Knowing that more than one might be needed for alternate takes and sequels, the designers installed a self-propagation mechanism in the crayfish. Unfortunately, they managed to jump into a wormhole and propagate themselves into an innumerable army of real-life nemeses. Thus, a virtual war became an actual one. Kame-kun is Japan's military response to this threat, but his knowledge of it is digitally honeycombed.

Barring these fantastical turns of events, Kame-kun's Japan feels stuck in a post-bubble, neocapitalist nostalgia. It is a nation still caught in the throes of a stereotypical obsession with technology and innovation while yearning for the insularity it enjoyed in former centuries. And while its block apartments, shopping districts, and crisp topography are no far cry from the present day, its dilapidated urban sectors and reliance on virtual technologies for travel speak of a ravaged society as much at war with itself as with its sworn enemies. Such dynamics are alive and well in Kame-kun's reality, where essentializing myths pit Japan as the "original" against "imitators" and view the postwar miracle as a metaphorical rebirth (Tatsumi 2006, 12). This rebirth has much to do with Japan's status as an occupied nation in the wake of the war. "Unstable as the postwar Japanese emperor system remains," writes Takayuki Tatsumi, "its deep structure bears the imprint of a false memory of democratic ideology; it is a system that revived the Japanese nation as one that had already developed a consistent, hardcore, democratic body politic, and as such it allowed the Japanese to survive the occupation peacefully" (17). Kame-kun can be seen as upholding this ideological dichotomy by being trapped in a cycle of self-awareness and compulsory weaponization.

The atmosphere of *Mr. Turtle* is indeed a throwback to postwar literature, in which the realm of Japanese SF assumed understandably vivid configurations following the nuclear attacks on Hiroshima and Nagasaki, Abe Kōbō's 1958 to 1959 serial *Inter Ice Age 4* (*Dai-Yon Kampyōki*) being a landmark example. The more-than-obvious implications thereof activate an authorial awareness of what Csicsery-Ronay calls the "nuclear sublime"—the awesome capacity for our most destructive technologies to obliterate creation at the molecular level. Csicsery-Ronay uses this term somewhat differently than Perry Miller's "technological sublime" (see Nye 1994), evoking not so much awe over as increasing immateriality of technological development toward ever more cerebral, internal, and invisible configurations: "Once the entire biosphere becomes vulnerable to engineered destruction . . . the most destructive physical might has been appropriated, and the once-sublime domain of nature seems to exist on human sufferance. The nuclear sublime is the catalyst for . . . awe and terror at the prospect that the war machine develops autonomously from mundane social concerns. Chained to the logic of the arms race, human engineers are no longer privileged actors at the forefront of history, but rather passive agents of techno-evolution's unfriendly experiments, only partially aware of what they're doing" (Csicsery-Ronay 2008, 159). If Kame-kun incarnates the fear of technological autonomy, as the remnant of a war fought by robots in place of humans for their mistakes, it is no wonder he should be subjected to discrimination. Because he was built to fight, his integration into society crosses a taboo line between producer and product and flags humans' attraction to violence.

Upon witnessing the bombing of Nagasaki, journalist William L. Laurence "saw the mushroom cloud as a prehistoric monster, and speculated that after a nuclear war, modern humans would devolve into an animal-like existence" (Hendershot 1999, 77). If we can imagine these sentiments being felt on both ends of the explosion, then the people of Kitano's near future must reconcile the cowardice of sending biomechanical stand-ins to air their dirty laundry. Kame-kun's existence, long after fulfilling its tactical purpose, invokes Laurence's fear of devolution. Kame-kun is a reminder to all who come to know him that, though wars on the outside come and go, those on the inside produce no victors.

Kame-kun is a creature of habit. The point of his existence is to wonder about the point of his existence. Daily walks are among his favorite activities, giving him leeway to connect the dots of his meager life into a recognizable image of earthly goings on. Kame-kun criticizes humans' penchant for invention even as he feels a kinship with them for having been designed in the image of the divine without being themselves divine. As a high-tech creation, he empathizes with this condition, spinning a web of inquiry around the self and its possible meanings in worlds beyond.

When we first meet Kame-kun, he is between jobs and moving into a new apartment. Throughout the novel, such attempts at fitting in disclose Japan's fundamental social resistance to his kind (even his landlady must check her own prejudices before handing him a key). After moving in, Kame-kun goes for a stroll to familiarize himself with the neighborhood and happens upon a riverbank just past the local train station. A group of ragtag kids sidles up alongside and kicks a soccer ball in his direction, hoping to knock him over. Kame-kun sustains the blow with his carapace and sends their ball into the river with a flick of his tail. Impressed by his strength but upset over losing their ball, one of the boys says, "[G]o back to Jupiter, you stupid turtle" (Kitano 2016, 4). This is our first hint of the epic war on Jupiter in which Kame-kun was once involved but of which he recalls the vaguest fragments. More important for the moment is the dual discrimination at play. Kame-kun is derogatorily marked by his apparent species, despite being an artificial simulacrum thereof, and by his warring past. The river is a metaphor for lost consciousness. Its ecosystem is familiar to him—or at least should be, given his reptilian design—but harbors as many mysteries as remnants of a life submerged.

Kame-kun knows humanity has co-opted animality to egotistical ends. In a chapter entitled "Shell," the reader learns of a recent trend among female high school students who wear turtle shells on their backs. Oddly enough, they favor the simple, single-keeled housings of the Japanese pond turtle and point derisively at Kame-kun for sporting the three keels characteristic of the Chinese pond turtle, now woefully out of fashion. Classifying his traits in this manner confirms a hierarchy of species and proves appearance matters. Later, it is explained that not only are girls *wearing* shells but they are also experimentally *bonded* to them in the hopes of increasing their lifespan. Kame-kun can only wonder whether his shell might not have had a previous owner and whether the flickers of his memory might not contain another's residuals.

Kame-kun's push for knowledge troubles the waters in which people admire their own reflections and asks whether humans must first lay claim to consensus before they can overcome it or whether the species, as a human concept to begin with, is just a distraction from the molecular sameness of things. Kame-kun seeks not the future but an honest look into the past. Even though he walks upright and works with his hands, he is not a humanoid robot, being no more human than the shell-toting high schoolers are animal. He is neither a traditional hero nor a goal-oriented individualist. The reader encounters him in a liminal state—not a point along a line but a line without a point. He does not build up the human; he breaks it down. Through his relentless information gathering (the result of his inherent desire for growth), he reduces the aura of life to a data stream. He sees the world not as a series of biorhythms but as one technological innovation in an eternity of others.

Mr. Turtle acknowledges the invisible forces of integration. Though humans continue to be the dominant species in *Mr. Turtle*, their fear of animals is so great that biomechanical production of them is the only method to which they can resort to keep them in check (even this backfires, as the crayfish ironically demonstrate). Therefore, Kame-kun's everyday life is not so much a battle of "human versus animal" as it is "inorganic versus hyperorganic." In this scheme, the organic functions as an adaptive language of behavioral consequence in those whose lives scroll by like so many lines of code.

As one born from war and who to war must return, Kame-kun serves the mutual exclusion of agency and passivity. His autonomy depends on the bioengineered energy of his able body, on both the active and inactive ingredients of his sustenance, and on the physics of this planet he calls home. His existence—a life consisting of little more than eating, working, and frequenting the local library to fuel his knowledge production—solves the equation of passivity by showing that his consciousness holds power by its general lack of consequence. It also denies the equation of agency with active being. His existence expands the possible spaces in which bodies make contact/retract, communicate/self-isolate, and injure/heal beyond the circumscription of normalized bodies, disabling the locks of anthropocentrism that have rusted around him.

Knowing One's Species World

One night, Kame-kun wakes up and looks out into the courtyard of his apartment complex. There, made visible by the full moon's light, he sees a mass of rodlike objects sticking out from the ground, each fitted with an eye. Their gaze changes him. Already the object of public scrutiny from speciesist humans, he feels compelled by this mysterious, nocturnal encounter to go further into the annals of history to better understand the reasons behind his creation. His quest for personal truth is not a neat analog to our own, even if it does share a contradiction of self-enhancement and -destruction.

Kame-kun's sense of self is distinctly chelonian. He sees the world as an accumulation of countless hexagons, which, like those of a turtle's shell, cleave an inner and outer realm. Because his shell is all he has, he believes the world moves with him. "God was to humans," the text muses, "as shells were to turtles" (16). Kame-kun reaches this epiphany during one of his walks near the library, which sits on an island in the river. The bridge leading to it is made of hexagonal stones, and the déjà vu of their shell-like pattern consumes him as he crosses it. Kame-kun is also quite fond of the library, a place where he can learn about himself by knowing the world. The library is an entity with its own color, scent, and kinesis. By reading books and watching videos, he gains gradual knowledge of how things work.

He grows fond of everyone who works there, especially a part-time archivist named Miwako, with whom he strikes up the novel's healthiest relationship. It so happens that Miwako is writing her graduate thesis on turtles. She understands Kame-kun better than he understands himself. When they first meet, she scans his shell and discovers it consists mainly of silicone and ceramic in thin, alternating layers. "It grows on its own, like crystal," she informs him, "in proportion to memory" (20). This reminds Kame-kun of the fact that he remembers nothing of the distant past, not least of all his relationship to the multiply referenced war on Jupiter. Miwako surmises those memories are classified.

Miwako's expository gifts to the reader are as profound as her emotional ones to Kame-kun. Through her, we learn our hero is a composite of manmade materials and living flesh. As someone who is "neither just hardware nor software" (96), Kame-kun is in a unique position to break a fourth wall that most animals cannot even crack. His unspoken mission is to give a voice to the voiceless, translating his inner animal for any who might benefit. His wisdom flourishes to educate himself before others—a key distinction from the purely allegorical animal. Though built as a weapon, Kame-kun enjoys the privilege of loading his mind and soul with less tangible ammunition.

Kame-kun's way of life offsets the tendency among humans to, by observing animals, become hyperaware of and locked into their own worlds. The biosemiotic triggers by which his behaviors unfold are rooted in physiological and psychological signs. From his perspective, life is a soft contradiction. He must hold down a job to eat and pay his rent. At the same time, he is aware of the impositions of his work. Around him, normality is static, antiprogressivist, and keeps him enclosed in a box branded with the traits of his species. Kame-kun follows the blueprint laid out for him by his creators even as he manages to elicit incredible diversity within its parameters. Kame-kun reframes his purview as nothing more than speciesism in a minor key, carving out a niche for human reasoning within his own. The latter is more than an implant because it thrives on self-generation. He is not, for the moment, conscripted into bare life. He lays life bare.

Kame-kun is always in the middle of things. The term by which Kitano refers to him is proof of this. He is neither a replicant (*repurika*) nor a turtle (*kame*), but a replican[t]urtle (*repurikame*). His affect is an internalization of effects from the outside and an externalization of effects from the inside. Being a turtle, he is always in his shell looking out, unable to transcend his half-domed world. At the same time, he knows there are endless worlds in other shells within him, just as he exists in another shell inside another, ad infinitum. The novel's narrator—who, we ultimately learn, is Kame-kun himself—shows great awareness of his species world even as he transcends it through the mechanism of trauma (something that cannot be preprogrammed). Jakob von Uexküll's elucidations are helpful here:

> No animal will ever leave its [own] space, the center of which is the animal itself. Wherever it goes, it is always surrounded by its own . . . space, filled with its own sensory spheres, irrespective of how much the objects change. Man [*sic*], on the other hand, when he wanders, tends to cut loose the space he moves in from his sensory spheres and thus to extend his paths in all directions. The vault of the sky gets higher and higher and the center of the world under the heavenly cupola is no longer himself but his home. Man does no longer move with a space that follows him faithfully, as his senses tell him, he moves instead in a space at

rest, a space that is cut loose from him and has its own center. Space has become autonomous as have the objects within it.

(2001, 109)

Kame-kun turns this conception on its head by embracing that awareness of infinity Uexküll attributes to humans alone and by navigating between human and animal realms with instinctive beauty. He need never intellectualize these transitions. Instead, he cultures them in himself and in others through the gifts of his thinking, his desires, and his work. As a cog in a larger machine, he challenges the myth of alienation through an intimate knowledge set by which he proves there is no such thing as space at rest.

Laboro, Ergo Sum

Upon meeting Kame-kun, the reader learns he has been laid off after a company buyout. The new management refuses to keep on a replican[t]urtle among its human employees. Prior to his forced resignation, Kame-kun receives a laptop as a parting gift from his manager. The laptop becomes the technological foundation of the novel and is, in fact, the very machine on which he has written it. Because Kame-kun does not talk (a weapon receives commands but does not give them), the laptop is his primary means of communication. With it, he can email, record his thoughts, and apply for his new job online. Without it, we would never know him.

Upon arriving for his job interview, he proceeds through a ruined landscape crumbling with vestiges of a world before the war. The area indicated on his application has fallen into use as a warehouse district. He rings the intercom. A middle-aged secretary answers and ushers him down a passageway to be interviewed by his future boss, Tsumiki. And yet, all Tsumiki wants to know is whether he can use a forklift. It so happens that Kame-kun has plenty of forklift experience. Tsumiki puts him through a trial run. Once Kame-kun slips into the pod that serves as a driver's seat, the hatch closes, and everything goes dark. It reminds him of being inside an egg, a feeling he realizes he has always known. He recognizes the usual controls, along with meters, panels, and screens he has never encountered. He feels like he knows these, too, and gets so lost in his oneness with the machine that he blacks out the first few times he operates it, as often happens in "mecha" anime and manga (Ikari Shinji, the human hero of *Neon Genesis Evangelion*, likewise blacks out when the cybernetic robot known as EVA Unit 01 lapses into berserk mode the first two times he tries to pilot it).

Mr. Turtle has a complicated relationship with technology. On the surface, it is practical and bare: forklifts, barcode scanners, and laptops speak of a world that, despite technical leaps, still operates on an early twenty-first-century level. The most advanced technology seems to have been encoded into Kame-kun himself and those he was bred to fight. He might easily have been programmed with all sorts of worldly knowledge but arrives on the scene of his daily life as a dam baring small cracks through which his past trickles with mounting force. He wonders why everything feels so familiar, as it did during his previous employment. The seat of his first forklift accommodated the curvature of his shell as if made for him, if not the other way around, and was the first indicator of a former life. The smoothness of his operational skills so amazed his human coworkers that they applauded and welcomed him into the blue-collar community. He excels in his new job, even as his labor teases out a forgotten past.

As a genre of estrangement, SF sheds valuable light on working economies. In his 1844 "On *The Jewish Question*," a young Karl Marx (2020) criticizes the (Christian) state for valorizing estrangement over man. Marx's essay draws a line between his early and later thinking along the issue of species-being, a concept that would recede from his best-known work, though its basic principle—that workers enable their own deterioration—would continue to be his red thread for decades. For Marx, productive life is species-life (i.e., humans being conscious of their species, a concept drawn from Ludwig Feuerbach). Animals produce only to satisfy their immediate needs without engaging in "abstract" labor, while humans lubricate functionality with aesthetic gel. Humans are unique in producing an actual material life through means of subsistence, but in doing so, they alienate their lives as a species. Technological determinism is only the dark of Kitano's novel, the light of which bears out in the fact that, as a product himself, Kame-kun has an "insider's view" of materialism. His labor is abstract for producing no commodity yet having social value in its protective mechanisms and allegiance to a whitewashed history.

As a use-oriented body, Kame-kun rounds Marx's sharper thinking on the point of labor economy. If Hegel wanted only liberation of mind and Marx that of real human beings, *Mr. Turtle* extends the trajectory by asking: What happens when products of human labor flirt with their own liberation?

Marx's species-life is not the life of a species, as determined by genetics and physical advantages. Rather, the species-life of human beings is the consummate political state where they sacrifice a direct connection to the self through the alienation of their labor, in turn supporting the superstructure that enables it. Species-life exists in opposition to material life as the *potential* of human nature and the ability to constitute one's activity. The animal throws a wrench into this thinking. As Sherryl Vint observes, "If we take seriously animals' capacity for social relations, then reducing their existence for beings-for-capital is a violation of their species-being as much as reducing humans to labour-power is a violation of ours" (2009, 124). More problematic for Vint than the reduction of labor-power is the proliferation of a system that would reduce *any* living creature to commodity status. The vicious cycle of production and alienation repeats along a border like that of Kame-kun's shell, in which the statuses of producer and produced are coterminous.

A detriment of this self-imagining is a lack of ability to imagine the self. The more one accedes to the parameters of species-being, the more one defers to the idea that a higher rate of production leads to a higher state of knowledge. Species-being is what Marx (2009) calls "estranged labor" in an 1844 essay of the same name. Like the estrangement of SF, Marx's estrangement is from our human bodies, our fellow laborers, and the commodities we produce and consume. Workers cannot be too conscious of themselves. This would be counterproductive, as their consciousness has been harnessed into the activity of labor, alienated from the products (which, to workers, are hostile) they help create. When labor comes to be alienated from production—that is, when the activity itself becomes alien—species-being has prevailed. Its truth is its fantasy: that we are universal and, therefore, free. Kame-kun actualizes a *conscious* relation to laboring beyond that of subsistence, all the while destabilizing the subject–object divide that weakens the integrity of subjecthood as it is optimistically defined in accord with social effects.

Eunjung Kim reworks this sentiment elsewhere when she says, "Certain bodies are oppressed not by 'thingification' . . . but by the specific mode of intelligibility with which the thing and other things are treated" (2012, 105). We might see the imposition of integrity on bodies as an objectification that fails to acknowledge the generative power of passivity. There is a necessary cocktail of agency and passivity in a discriminated subject like Kame-kun, who is perceived to be a "less-than" in relation to the "must-haves." His passivity regarding labor is just as active as his desire to uncover repressed memories and understand the fallacy of his species-being. Returning to Marx's "Estranged Labor," we find that "[m]an is a species-being, not only because in practice and in theory he adopts the species (his own as well as those of other things) as his object, but . . . also because he treats himself as the actual, living species; because he treats himself as a *universal* and therefore a free being." Conversely, being for all intents and purposes an animal, Kame-kun has no access to the same sort of universality as his human coworkers. He must find his own creative, pseudo-scientific solutions to existential crises.

As a cyborg, Kame-kun challenges universal personhood. Given his thoughts on humanity and God, he is far more interested in the philosophical radiations of his inbuilt practicalities and in the neural mechanisms that push him to seek regular employment than in the fate of humankind. In such a context, Marx's communism cannot proliferate around the eradication of personality in favor of a collective self but an abolition of private property, which, for Marx and Engels (2005, 60n), refers to private control of economy, not personal possessions. Kame-kun is aware that the true alien, "to whom labor and the product of labor belongs, in whose service labor is done and for whose benefit the product of labor is provided, can only be *man* himself" (original emphasis), or, in his case, the *turtle* himself. Kame-kun's lack of interest in commodities paws at the theory that buying products (commodities fetish) is about reinforcement of the estrangement of labor. The secret, as Marx would have it, of private property is that "on the one hand it is the *product* of alienated labor, and that on the other it is the *means* by which labor alienates itself, *the realization of this alienation*" ("Estranged," original emphases). Whether consciously or not, Kame-kun lives this secret to the fullest.

Kame-kun is an unwanted other—what Marxists might call a "stateless creature"—destined to a life of never fitting in. The fact that turtles once manufactured for war are "allowed" to become functioning members of human society hints at an ethical aversion to destroying them outright, even if they are only being kept alive so they might be deployed at a moment's notice for future conflicts, as happens in the novel's final act. The state exploits replican[t]urtles to bandage its flaws. Though Kame-kun may not see himself as a product of capitalist development, he knows capitalist development co-opts the animal sphere by polluting and destroying the environment. He is triply alienated by work, self, and society, hyperbolically reimagined by way of anti-turtle discrimination. As Haraway (1994, 97) suggests, however, "[t]o be constituted by another's desire is not the same thing as to be alienated in the violent separation of the laborer from his product." Because the fluidity of sociopolitical life in Kitano's Japan rests on the shoulders of cyborgs, any alienation felt by Kame-kun can only come from within because he turns every life event in his mental hands like a Rubik's cube until its colors begin to unify.

In Marx's estimation, "the more universal man (or the animal) is, the more universal is the sphere of inorganic nature on which he lives," meaning man embraces both organic and inorganic objects as part of his totality of conscious being, and that "[t]he universality of man appears in practice precisely in the universality which makes all nature his *inorganic* body—both inasmuch as nature is (1) his direct means of life, and (2) the material, the object, and the instrument of his life activity. Nature is man's *inorganic* body—nature, that is, insofar as it is not itself human body. Man *lives* on nature—means that nature is his body, with which he must remain in continuous interchange if he is not to die. That man's physical and spiritual life is linked to nature means simply that nature is linked to itself, for man is a part of nature." Marx goes on to say the worker "only feels himself freely active in his animal functions—eating, drinking, procreating, or at most in his dwelling and in dressing-up, etc.; and in his human functions he no longer feels himself to be anything but an animal. What is animal becomes human and what is human becomes animal" (Marx, "Estranged," original emphases). Speculative fiction approaches this from another angle. Whereas the industrial world fears humans becoming machines, the hyper-modern world fears machines becoming humans. Kame-kun's hands are described not as those of a real turtle but as precision instruments designed to handle various tasks with ease. His laboring body resonates with skills analogous to those of humans, whose own skills are modeled off nature. It is not that Kame-kun becomes something other than self but that his autonomous self threatens to replace the worker-being he was created to be.

Determining what constitutes the alienation of labor for a cyborg turtle requires one to redefine the Marxist concept of labor when the laborer is neither human nor animal. It cannot be that Kame-kun's labor is external to him because, as an agent of nature, his laboring abilities are hardwired. Neither can it be that his labor is forced because, as one calibrated to excel in it, he is inseparable from his need to work. He is living proof that "animals can be alienated from their species-being as much as humans can be from ours" (Vint 2009, 130). His desire *is* the work and cannot be anyone else's. His paradigmatic functions align with Marx only when he is being used as a weapon of mass destruction, when his labor is external by force. Kame-kun is more than an animal, "immediately one with its life activity," whereas "[m]an makes his life activity itself the object of his will and of his consciousness" ("Estranged"). The cruel allure of estranged labor is that it tricks human beings into thinking their consciousness allows them to forge their own life path as a way of justifying existence through self-sustenance. For Kame-kun, it is more than a dichotomy between the externality of production versus the internality of self-constitution, for if political economy hides the estrangement of labor, then personal economy can turn on a black light to make it glow. The worker and worker's deterioration are also being produced in the labor process and, in Kame-kun's case, are courting repressed trauma as the flower courts the bee.

In volume 1 of *Capital*, Marx says "sensuous characteristics" must be absent in the product so that the end products seem to us "abounding in metaphysical subtleties and theological niceties" (cited in Vint 2016, 104). Indeed, Kame-kun echoes the idea that "[t]he worker can create nothing without *nature*, without the *sensuous external world*. It is the material on which his labor is realized, in which it is active, from which, and by means of which it produces." Increased appropriation of nature leads to negation of the self. Consequently,

> the more the worker by his labor *appropriates* the external world, sensuous nature, the more he deprives himself of the *means of life* in two respects: first, in that the sensuous external world more and more ceases to be an object belonging to his labor—to be his labor's *means of life*; and, second, in that it more and more ceases to be a *means of life* in the immediate sense, means for the physical subsistence of the worker. In both respects, therefore, the worker becomes a servant of his object, first, in that he receives an *object of labor*, i.e., in that he receives *work*, and, secondly, in that he receives *means of subsistence*. This enables him to exist, first as a worker; and second, as a *physical subject*. The height of this servitude is that it is only as a *worker* that he can maintain himself as a *physical subject* and that it is only as a *physical subject* that he is a worker.
>
> (Marx, "Estranged," original emphases)

It is under the sign of these cosmologies that Petrus Liu follows the logic of hegemony in the formation of the subject, seeing the intersection of cultural and economic forces not in the laboring body but in the units of time under which that body's productive activities come to be measured. Because there is no universal conception of time or value attached to time, one must not be mistaken in thinking that all labors are "morally equivalent" (Liu 2012, 71). In this spirit, Liu questions the irreconcilability of the young and mature Marx, from liberal rationalism to communalist humanism, freedom *from* to community *within*. It is not a simple matter of pitting humanism against posthumanism, for not only is the human objectified, commoditized, and mechanized through labor processes, but there is also an attendant reverse anthropomorphism, "an ideological process whereby unequal relations between human beings take on the appearance of an equitable exchange between things" (75) and whereby material things are humanized to divert consumers' attention from their origins.

This is what Liu is getting at when he writes, "Since the human is not a universally identical condition but a privileged status differentially and hierarchically produced across temporal and spatial sites of power, it has become politically and ethically imperative for poststructuralists to pluralize the human" (76). In short, poststructuralists have largely failed to own up to their disinterest in humanity. Once self-reflection is knocked from its perch, its wings prove useless. As a novel about Japan, *Mr. Turtle* thrives on its disruption of Eurocentric humanism and reframes a fundamental quandary: It is not whether the independence granted to human subjects is available or not to nonhuman subjects but that independence is not even available to human subjects to begin with, so long as they are enmeshed in a system that fuels the illusion of independence and freedom available to all. Kitano reminds his readers of Kame-kun's subhuman status as a cognizant relic of war while touting the replican[t]urtle's ability to overcome estrangement by being, in essence, a sentient form of capital.

Kame-kun walks necessary lines of difference. His social construction is living proof of the dialectical relationship between industrial capitalism and socialism, as well as between species and technologies. Similarly, labor processes are natural *and* social, for while past labor is not always present in the labor process, it comes back to haunt Kame-kun with a vengeance. He may use machines to aid his production, where the machine would normally reorganize the demands of the human body in relation to work, but as a machine himself, Kame-kun is awakened to the fullness of his military past. Machinery creates no new value; it only transfers it.

Technology runs on the relationship between humans and nature. It also mediates that relationship. But when the worker is technology incarnate, he signifies an awareness of his becoming and validates that awareness by existing. Like a tape recorder placed in a box and turned on to document the sounds of its internal mechanisms, he archives the voices of his past within the container of the physical world. Kame-kun becomes an unwitting agent of what Thomas Hobbes called *bellum omnium contra omnes* ("the war of all against all") when the novel begins to frame his work as "combat." Kame-kun wonders about this as the company secretary explains to him the fundamental danger and purpose of his work: While inventorying every container that arrives at the warehouse, he is to summarily destroy any large crayfish-like biomechanoids found waiting inside, as these were his sworn enemies during the war. Considering the mastery with which he dispatches these creatures, Kame-kun can no longer deny he has ever been to Jupiter.

But at what point does the "natural" become "unnatural?" How far can one take the metaphor of nature before it degrades? If all manufactured objects begin as raw materials drawn from the ground, at what point do they become artificial through modification? This is, I suspect, the point Marx was trying to make when he described human bodies as bearing traces of their physical and socioeconomic pasts. What does it mean to say that everything is unnatural? Does this not simply reverse the scale without recalculating what is being measured? *Mr. Turtle* is not about transcending humanity but about the persistence of relying on technology-as-animal to absorb—and inflict—the consequences of its errors. After all, Marx was concerned with humanity's ability to build up and alienate itself, leaving animals to forage for scraps across the factory floor. Animals were always analogic scavengers.

Kame-kun embodies dominant social expectations and stereotypes of the working class but also the power of the android to transcend them. Because replican[t]urtles are impervious to death, making them more effective in battle, Kame-kun's forklift is itself a giant robotic turtle, hardwired to hunger for the crayfish it devours, to the extent that Kame-kun likens the aftermath of his vicarious gorging to a battlefield. That he can approach these "savage" acts from the vantage point of self-reflection in the context of controlled labor means his cognizance is bound to privilege, secondhand though it might be, upgraded from thoughtless (re)actions on the battlefront. Labor echoes national trauma, as when Kame-kun needs an air conditioning unit in his apartment fixed and returns home to find the electricians wreaking havoc on the unit they have come to fix. As they kick and maim the hapless machine, which crawls by means of living legs, they explain that its former owner had stolen it from a military research facility. In taking out their aggression on the machine in mock battle, they are diffusing their responses to the war. These incidents, despite being comic relief, are outlets for repressions and show that at least some wounds of the war are still fresh in the dermis of the larger social imaginary.

By its end, *Mr. Turtle* may be read two ways from a Marxist angle: either as a cautionary tale of neocapitalist angst or as an undermining of Marxist values through the transformation of alienation into hybrid futures that are anything but utopian. The crayfish Kame-kun battles daily are a crisis of productive (if not production) error, a parthenogenetic nightmare in which he always comes out on top. Like the scripts he must follow, piped in from the film studio who designed those crayfish to act within certain parameters, he counts his value by the word, even as he veers from what is written in acts of bold, personal expression, ever in service of the tasks at hand.

Storehouses of Memory

Ideologies in *Mr. Turtle* are plastic. Consider Kitano's "Tower of Progress" (*Shinpo no Tō*), a monument made in the image of a man for an international expo, since converted into a museum. Only after working at the warehouse for some time does Kame-kun realize his place of work is connected to the museum. Tsumiki explains it was once called the "Tower of Progress and Harmony" but that the war has broken any illusions of peace such a name entails. The tower displays its public power most visibly in the museum, the name of which has also changed, from "National Museum" to "War Museum." The museum is so vast and random that even Kame-kun gets lost in its corridors. His job is to inventory the underground storehouses under a curator's watchful eye. Kame-kun conducts his work as methodically as possible so as not to disturb the museum's patrons. On days when no goods arrive, he takes to sorting things, having no idea on which laws or rules their organization is based. An unruly AI system handles all the exhibition materials and is, in fact, one of them (having been once used, like Kame-kun, as a tactical weapon).

A new museum installation called the "Great Battlefield Panorama" means to recreate as faithfully as possible the war on Jupiter. Debate continues to rage among the exhibition's advisors (who see the war as finished but the aftermath everlasting) and its consultants (who cite its glorification of unilateral aggression). They reach a compromise in the form of the final exhibition, which offers simulations of takeoff, battle, and hypersleep. As a part of this archive, Kame-kun becomes aware that he has been indirectly aiding in making it more real, as the raw combat data of his crayfish encounters is being fed into the panorama's mock combat engine. Even in the novel's near future, no one can say for sure whether virtual reality is consummate or an empty mirror of our own. "On the other hand," the story goes on, "by managing this virtual space, one can affect reality," and "all acts of war have come to be played out in virtual space" (Kitano 2016, 74). From a television special, Kame-kun further learns why turtles were the chosen form of his kind:

Reason #1: *They can hibernate.*
Reason #2: *Their shells allow them to withstand high speeds and impacts.*
Reason #3: *They are long-lived. Many get to be older than humans. As a result, they are especially patient.*
Reason #4: *They will eat anything.*
Reason #5: *They're aesthetically pleasing. Even those who profess to hate reptiles tend to be fine with turtles. They're also popular among women and children.*

(118)

Replican[t]urtles differ from real ones in that they walk upright on their hind legs, use both hands, and inhabit composite shells. The video's narrator explains that replican[t]urtles favor apples to supplement their vitamin and fiber deficiencies.

When Kame-kun arrives at work one day, he notices Tsumiki talking with a stranger. Tsumiki introduces him as a representative of the turtle manufacturer who saw Kame-kun on TV and was curious to meet him in person. After confirming that Kame-kun is in working condition, he tells Tsumiki, "Because he's in reset mode, so long as he doesn't over-exert himself I foresee no problems allowing him to stay on here—until such time as the next mission can be determined" (135). Meanwhile, the library-as-storehouse gives Kame-kun an opportunity for Kitano to indulge in his own fascination with the canon of SF. Building on her interest in turtles, Miwako has been studying Kame-kun's shell with the intent of mapping what is inside of it. While waiting, Kame-kun reads up on the classics. He takes out two books. One is Arthur C. Clarke's *2010: Odyssey Two* (1982), and the other is on the making of the film

(1986, directed by Peter Hyams) of the same name. He stays at the library until all the patrons have gone to allow Miwako to conduct her experiment. She attaches probes and electrodes to his shell, feeds them into a laptop computer, and activates them. His shell becomes warm, and he begins to experience waking dreams. He has a vision in which Miwako removes her clothes and stands before him naked, baring a shell on her back in the shape of two folded wings. Mention of Clarke is no coincidence, as *Mr. Turtle* questions the past like *2001: A Space Odyssey* (1968) questions the future. And just as the ending of Stanley Kubrick's 1968 film adaptation was a regression into our ultimate, prebirth past, so does Kame-kun regress into (and beyond) the inner world of his shell, mapping layers of himself onto Miwako's body.

Kame-kun's memories belong not to him but to his shell—or, more precisely, to the shell's previous wearer. Recollections overlap with the present until the two become indistinguishable. The knowledge of another world has been sleeping inside him all along, and it has taken a dream to awaken it. In an induced trance state, sentences from his laptop float before him, each describing one mundane aspect of his life after another. And as everything comes crashing down on him, he realizes the world inside his shell is being quickly overwritten.

He then receives an email from another turtle. It gives only a date and meeting place and says that he must prepare for hibernation. He wonders whether the message might have come from inside his shell after all. He moves out of his apartment and quits his job. He goes to the library to return his books, only to discover that Miwako is on indefinite research leave. This surprises him but makes his imminent transition far easier to accept. As outlined in the email, he is being deployed to a launching site at Tanegashima to enter a state of hibernation and be rocketed off to Jupiter. Rather than feel used by the system, Kame-kun looks forward to the prospect of meeting other turtles.

The last possession he removes from his bag is his laptop. He opens the screen slowly, caresses the keyboard, and types out the first heading of the novel itself: "Chapter 1: Replican[t]urtle." He keeps typing, telling everything we have just read before it vanishes from his memory bank. He walks as far as the library and drops the laptop into the return slot, then turns away empty-handed. Because he utters not a single word throughout the novel, it is the only way in which he might still be recognized for his sentience, his will to live, and his worldview.

In a story that lacks any explicit spiritual overlay, Kame-kun fills in the paternal gap left by capitalism. Despite being infantilized by humans, he is anything but abject, stimulated by inklings of romance, purpose, and socioeconomic value. *Mr. Turtle* is what Stanisław Lem (cited in Moulthrop and Grigar 2017, 2) would call "bitic" literature, by which a work's creator "may have been the author indirectly . . . but performing the functions which generated the real author's acts of creation." As Alan Liu (cited in Moulthrop and Grigar 2017, 50) puts it: "Where once the job of literature and the arts was creativity, now, in an age of total innovation, I think it must be history. That is to say, it must be a special, dark kind of history. The creative arts as cultural criticism (and vice versa) must be the history not of things created—the great, auratic artifacts treasured by a conservative or curatorial history—but of things destroyed in the name of creation." Such cyclicity valorizes a feedback loop of which Kame-kun will forever be a part.

Between (Electric) Animals and Androids

In the third section of *Mr. Turtle*, Kame-kun befriends a cat that has been hanging around his apartment complex after being scared off by a military operation not far away. Upon noticing Kame-kun looking up information about cats at the library, Miwako proceeds to tell him at some length about a part-time job she once had, meticulously tracking and recording cat populations living on a small island. "The domesticated cat," she explains, "is a creature of habit. It will rarely deviate from an established routine" (Kitano 2016, 80). Kame-kun sees his life in the same way: as a matter of routine. Miwako tells him cats love chicken breast, so he buys some to lure the cat into his apartment. When he lays out his futon, the cat gets into bed with him, snuggling against him so tightly that it feels as though the cat is trying to slip into his shell.

Around this time, Kame-kun ramps up his interest in recovering memories of Jupiter. Miwako tells him those memories are locked somewhere in his shell, like a dream he cannot recall. In response, Kame-kun types a single sentence on his laptop: *Do turtle shells dream of turtles?* Peering over his shoulder, Miwako chimes in, "*Do Androids Dream of Electric Sheep?*" (102, hereafter, *Electric Sheep*), naming Philip K. Dick's 1968 classic, without which *Mr. Turtle* might not have been written. Is it coincidental that Dick's novel (1996, 2) should begin with the following, republished from a 1966 issue of *Reuters*?

> Auckland: A turtle which explorer Captain Cook gave to the king of Tonga in 1777 died yesterday. It was nearly 200 years old. The

animal, called Tu'Imalila, died at the royal palace ground in the Tongan capital of Nuku, Alofa. The people of Tonga regarded the animal as a chief and special keepers were appointed to look after it. It was blinded in a bush fire a few years ago. Tonga radio said Tu'Imalila's carcass would be sent to the Auckland museum in New Zealand.

The reader has no initial context for this anecdote but soon discovers that real animals are hard to come by in Dick's imaginary future. Animals and their robotic simulacra are central in ways they are not in director Ridley Scott's 1982 film adaptation, *Blade Runner*. Incidentally, Kitano claims to have been inspired more by the film than the novel, which makes sense given that *"Blade Runner* was welcomed in Japan because it reenacted for viewers both their own false memories of democracy and the hybrid construction of their postwar selves" (Tatsumi 2006, 20). Rick Deckard, an android bounty hunter, lives in an era where humans have become an endangered species. He and his wife are the dissatisfied owners of an electric sheep and pine for the day when they might have the real thing. Having an animal of either kind is a social necessity in the wake of the catastrophe known as World War Terminus, brought on by a toxic dust that has pushed humanity off the planet and all but destroyed low-class survivors from the inside out. Deckard's sheep is like a living Natsume simulation, susceptible to sickness and starvation. This fallacy of upkeep causes Deckard to hate the animal, which he sees as possessing the "tyranny of an object" (Dick 1996, 42). He must nurture it, or it will die along with the illusion of his pastoral power.

Libraries in Deckard's world house a colonial archive containing all that is left of times before. Their existence is a trauma in and of itself that funnels millennia of violence, the significance of which has been obliterated by Terminus. *Mr. Turtle* may not feel quite so dystopian, but it sympathizes with this point insofar as the library is Kame-kun's largest window into the self. Just as Deckard ponders the significance of the electric animal, which he begrudgingly sees as either an "inferior robot" or an "evolved version of the ersatz animal" (42), Kame-kun balances advancement and constructed purpose on the fulcrum of his existence.

Kame-kun shares another aspect with Deckard's victims. As one of the androids in Dick's novel puts it to the bounty hunter: "It's a chance anyway, breaking free and coming here to Earth, where we're not even considered animals. Where every worm and wood louse is considered more desirable than all of us put together" (122). Laying a transparency of this statement over *Mr. Turtle*, we might conclude that Kamekun's discrimination has less to do with being a turtle and more to do with being a replicant. His existence flies in the face of nature, and he must watch as humans appropriate the sacred shells of his kind, wearing them as embellishments to an already-dominant species.

Dick's androids have it even tougher. As the "mobile donkey engine[s] of the colonization program" and, more derogatorily, "a menace to the pristine heredity of the [human] race" (16), they must be aware of their service to the human empire, which has spread its social virus to the terra of Mars. Though both are the targets of discomfort and negativity, Dick's androids are resentful toward their creation, while Kame-kun is quietly resigned to his. Separating humans from androids and animals is their capacity for empathy, as opposed to intelligence, which "to some degree could be found throughout every phylum and order" (30). Androids, Deckard concedes, are different from electric animals for being, at least, organic and alive. Kame-kun is unique for being both.

In this context, empathy exists in opposition to what Dick calls a "flattening of affect" (37), the sometimes sudden apathy of android countenance when confronted with the AI determination test administered by bounty hunters or, in extreme cases, imminent death. The labeling of empathy, however, discloses two problems. First, empathy implies an ineluctable and hierarchical difference between the empathizer and whatever is being empathized. Empathy ensures that hierarchy never succumbs to violence (e.g., the killing of rogue androids). Second, empathy tightens the ideological screws of its definition. Because empathy in *Electric Sheep* has been pathologically reduced to a fixed number of quantifiable variables, it is firmly within the control of those it most benefits. Its underlying power structures can hardly be challenged in a system that rewards those who unquestioningly swallow it, even if, at heart, empathy best speaks to the vast interconnections between groups.

When Deckard fuses with spiritual figurehead Wilbur Mercer via the so-called empathy box, Mercer tells him in a vision: "It is the basic condition of life, to be required to violate your own identity" (179). In those words, Deckard has learned that true empathy must involve killing not only androids devoid of it but also something in himself. Mercer's pseudo-religious rhetoric cradles a core contradiction: "As long as some creature experienced joy, then the condition for all other creatures included a fragment of joy. However, if any living being suffered, then for all the rest the shadow could not be entirely cast off" (31). Only when suffering, in even the slightest form, echoes like a shout from a mountaintop does its transformative potential become possible.

Toward the novel's end, Deckard has dispatched the androids assigned to him: "In the early morning light the land below him extended seemingly forever, gray and refuse-littered. Pebbles the size of houses had rolled to a stop next to one another, and he thought, It's like a shipping room when all the merchandise has left. Only fragments of crates remain, the containers which signify nothing in themselves" (228). This image presages the warehouses of *Mr. Turtle*, in which Kame-kun must sift through vestiges of destructive pasts to assemble a cohesive version for future generations. When Deckard, in a Mercer-induced vision, becomes aware of what he calls "inconspicuous life" (238), he does not simply open an internal line of communication to other species; he opens an external channel of humility toward the world they inhabit. "Thus to be a living creature," says one interpreter, "to have real authenticity, to fulfill the demands of empathy, and understand his humanity, Deckard must absent himself from his own being" (Berman 2008, 127). To understand the other, he must disconnect the self.

In Deckard's lifetime, animals have become more sacred because they embody a rarity of frequency that takes on "original" status in a carbon-copy world. The illusion maintained by mechanical animals, too, is sacred. For their human caretakers, animals have only negligibly changed in social position (their increased currency exists to stabilize the human). Neither has the incorporation of androids into daily life changed the subhuman position of their organic counterparts. Rather, it has shored up that position (keeping the animal sacred keeps its status clear) as a subservient one, which, despite the overcompensation of conservational tendencies, reinforces the human project through disdain toward and economic need for artificial life. While Kame-kun is, as Dick (1996) would put it, an "organic android," he is an amalgamation of human and animal signatures and is endowed with sentience, self-awareness, and a capacity for communication and original thought with which none of Dick's animals are endowed. Terminus was needlessly fought as a means of assigning blame to a blameless compromise of human life by the radioactive dust belched from Earth's gut. Because nature is without discrimination, humans continually fill that emptiness with denial and reactionary countermeasures. The war in *Mr. Turtle* is a typical one, even if its cause is unclear. Played out as exercises in determination, battles of animals are little more than self-projections of national interests.

Tripping Points

The marginalization of any object is a negation of its being in the world. Regardless of whether androids are "alive," their survival imparts languages of agency to passive tongues. *Mr. Turtle* describes our relationship with technology as already posthuman. In a developed world where the habitus (or lifeworld, as phenomenologists would have it) reigns supreme, where even the most uncanny entities scream with familiarity, androids represent a viable method of emancipation. Kitano is showing that humans celebrate exclusivity without realizing they live in a world saturated with hybridity.

No amount of deconstruction can erase the power of dialectical reasoning. More important than abolition is the blurring of those categories. The binaries are not expendable but constantly re-harmonized to the tune of circumstance. If the body can be a victim of biopolitics, it can also be a discursive agent in a "potent field of operations" (Haraway 1994, 101). The cyborg, ever nonnormative, can only be a political simulacrum because its programming will always bear the motivations of its creators, even if it makes choices within that system. Its identity will be light as a feather when weighed against its self-protective instincts. Kame-kun protects himself not to lock in his identity but so that this incarnation of his identity might be remembered.

Mr. Turtle makes a nuanced point about transhumanism, which burdens android populations with the human fear of death. By uploading the parameters of consciousness into biomechanical bodies, technicians fill those internal arenas of artificial intelligence with their own unresolvable humanity and impossible dreams. Kame-kun stands in not for humanity but for animality. Some interpret *Mr. Turtle* as a thinly veiled allegory of work and retirement, but the author begs to disagree and, in spite of the novel's references to popular anime and mecha subculture, claims to have been evoking the integrity of the common novel more than the ethos of the anime generation (see Sasabe 2001).

Kame-kun is an artificially intelligent product. His pathways verge and merge, evoking times and spaces without physical interface. Like his typewritten diary, he sprouts nerves of fibrous sincerity, signaling countless other lives in countless other universes. Memories may be wiped and bodies may decompose, but the story moves until it finds new ones to inhabit. Humans, animals, and objects are all susceptible to migration. They need not ever hurt one another except by the accident of chance while tripping over their own shadows.

Postanimalism
A Conclusion

> "Meanwhile, if as a utopist (indeed), I hate what
> I am figuring out, I think that there is hope."
>
> —Nassim Nicholas Taleb (2014, 79)

In the preceding chapters, I have discussed ways in which one might tease out "productive errors" slithering through contemporary Japanese literature amid a trending desire to think with animals. In folding posthumanist impulses into the dough of my analysis, I originally intended to leaven Japanese literary studies with the notion of productive error. Instead, I found that productive error had been a vital ingredient all along. The errors with which I am most enamored invite a broader conversation. But error is not a key that unlocks total understanding. It is, rather, the hole into which that key is inserted, a space that, depending on how one looks at it, either mimics a smudge of darkness against the vastness of a door or an unfathomable abyss of possibility threatening to consume that door. The point of this book is not to solve problems (any such claim would extend the tracks of denial from which I have been at great pains to derail) but to admit complicity in historically potent errors that deserve more careful attention.

The writings I have subjected to scrutiny constitute a composite genre by force of my suggestion, but in them is the potential to be taken as affirmative in recognition of their damage. The writers behind these texts have done a forthright thing. Rather than flock to narrative staples by romanticizing animals to a point so far from their species that traits fade in favor of an anthropomorphic fallacy, they have gone willfully into the thick of resistance to see what might be gleaned from its bram-ble. No one understood this better than Bandō Masako, whose "Killing Kittens" is an engorged tick not likely to be tweezed anytime soon.

A traditional reading of Bandō's essay would take it in the way it is presented: as confession. Readers who have already made up their minds about animals, who dabble in respect for nonhuman life to feel they have done their part, or who believe so wholeheartedly in the subjective importance of animals that, for them, animals are worthy of worship, thereby freeing them from responsibility, will likely see her text as a terri-fying admission and a personal attack on their ethical worldview. In this respect, Bandō can only have been sarcastic when she wrote, "the pain and grief that come from killing are mine alone to bear" (2009, 71), for her moral strategy is to highlight precisely the opposite. The pain and grief of killing, rather, cue the responsibility of all who read "Killing Kittens" to determine how they fit into the grander flight hidden in its short wingspan. It is for this cause that Bandō's kittens, lifeless as they might be, represent the hypocrisy of a neoliberal sympathy. I read their possible demise not as a tragedy of ignorance but as a mirror lifted to it.

Guide-dog literature occupies a corollary band of the productive error spectrum in which one loves animals so much that their individuality is brightened to blinding levels. This literature shows a side of humanity that is both loving and abusive. *Berna's Tail* is a poignant read. In the con-text of Japan's disability histories, however, its moral imperatives lose potency. It is neither my position nor intention to blame Gunji Nanae for writing her autobiography, in which she shares the pros and cons of her dual affliction, being blind and reliant on a guide dog in a society unprepared to accept either. Those closest to her learn to deal with their own errors. Whether or not this literature has the power to repair the infrastructure of social systems toward inclusivity remains to be seen and warrants further examination with this question in mind.

Otsuichi and Stephen King fall into the same trap from the other direction. Like the immovable Bandō, they realize readers must recog-nize the terrifying aspects of human–pet relationships and the pains one endures in taking those aspects to heart. For anyone frightened by the very idea of such stories—one who would shed thoughtful, and surely genuine, tears over the death of a pet whose life brought fulfill-ment to humans—the morose fulfillment of King's reanimated cat must feel like a root canal without anesthesia. At least *real* pets, one might say, live under the protection of love and give nothing less than love in return. While it may be futile to argue with this logic in principle, it does one well to recognize the truths activated by the relationships King and Otsuichi have so gruesomely portrayed. Genuinely loving animals, they seem to say, is knowing when to let go of them.

These authors chose their paths because they were honest in recognizing the ruptures inherent in their task. Whether one sides with Bandō for admitting her role in the contradictions of urban life or with Gunji for admitting her treatment of a dog as a prosthesis, they have traced idiosyncratic proclivities to logical ends. Purely symbolic animals do not require this sort of intellectual labor; they distort reality so that it can be reclaimed as such. Such is the endurance of an archetype.

Kitano Yūsaku's *Mr. Turtle* is something of a rescue narrative. In Kame-kun's circuitry, enmeshed with organic flesh and proteins, beats the signal of one who lives to question his aliveness. The more one reads of his quotidian life, the more one realizes that neither his humanity *nor* his animality matter. This is what makes Kame-kun so progressive: He shows us what questions can look like when taking on lives on their own. Kitano's novel exposes the hypocrisy of posthumanism swirling around the other side of the motherboard. Kame-kun meets the values humans ascribe to speech, social contribution, and war. Above all, he exposes our evangelical allegiance to memory and remembrance. Kame-kun cannot escape this urge as he frantically types out an autobiographical sketch before his memory is wiped.

While Kame-kun is subjected to a level of misunderstanding and discrimination rivaled only by his own self-scrutiny, he is content with an unremarkable life. He takes greatest pleasure in the simplest activities—making use of the library or finding a warm spot to sunbathe—and manages to develop a real connection with Miwako, whose interest in him may or may not be purely scientific. Even those closest to Kame-kun may see him as nothing more than what he is, though he transcends those barriers of expectation when he fantasizes about Miwako as a love object. Most humans, in their fierce dependence on technology and communication, treat him like another machine—or worse, an animal. He responds by confronting them with the illicitness lurking behind their proper facades.

That is, until he begins to "speak" their language through his laptop. Armed with that tool, he inspires a sense of care in others, ranging from the admiration of his former and current managers to his landlady and even the one who manufactured him for service. Reassessments of his character seep into Kitano's self-reflective postscript as well. The author admits to modeling the neighborhood in which Kame-kun lives off his own. When considering this place as a setting for a novel, he recalls asking himself: "Would this be an appropriate place for Kame-kun?" (Kitano 2016, 166). We might as well pose similar questions when reading any piece of animal literature: Is this an appropriate altar for the animal in question? Should there be an altar at all?

If it feels difficult to navigate these implications, it is because they are framed by and bound to a secular language. In this sense, animality is something with which one cannot ever claim total alliance. To embrace it as something to which we automatically belong is to focus on the moon and call it the sun. The binary shifts but does not separate. That is why I end here by advocating what I call "postanimalism," an undermining of the necessitarianism of our relationships with animals, by which mechanisms of grief industrialize individual care for and mass destruction of nonhuman lives. There is nothing beyond these relationships because we are their progeny, indefinitely redrawing their circles in denial of anything that segments them. Were the maintenance of the status quo not so important, entire regimes would not be designed to reinscribe them through education, agriculture, and industry.

If posthumanism is understood to be a radical enmeshment of bioforms and inanimates, then it necessarily relies on species narcissism and denial of error. By this I mean to suggest that posthumanism is essentially human in its allegiance to morally high-grounded politics. Postanimalism is the next logical step toward the realization of an interspecies world. It entails not only a flip of its counterpart—that is, it is about more than expanding animality to include humanity—but also a testimony of our treatment of animals as egomorphic images.

It is in the service of postanimalism that I ordered the stories in the way that I did, for their context and construction are as important as their situations. The breeding and keeping of pets—and, for that matter, the manufacturing and production of cyborg turtles—may be sullied, as Bandō suggests, by capitalist greed, but it is a noble pursuit that showcases the best of humanity for those so inclined. The breeding of animals allows humans to be more selective than they might be allowed to be with humans, even if it springs from a desire to express perfection and communion with all species. We are sorely misguided if we think we are solving the problem by denouncing breeder-manufacturers. We cannot direct our attentions toward the stewards of effect without interrogating those of cause.

The Japanese writings I have chosen all reach for the ideal of unity, as much a belief system as the arguments leveled against it. At stake here is not the loyalty, love, or intelligence of animals but rather our wayward perceptions of those traits. To blame authors—especially those, like Gunji, who write from personal experience—for overromanticizing their relationships with animals is to deny the truth of those relationships for the authors and to ignore their grappling with error. Our job should not be to do away with personal truths but to recognize their function as idols.

Postanimalism recognizes the productive errors not only of texts but also of our reactions to them. Any animal story need not conform to the grander implications of species existence. Despite Gunji's thoughts on the plight of blind people in Japan, her book is more concerned with her relationship to the guide dog, Berna, whose own phenomenological existence is closest to Gunji's for being born of necessity. Whatever the scale involved, nature is paramount. All of this requires a method of imagining. Postanimalism attends to this storytelling urge and moves it beyond the threshold of circumstance into universal truth (or so it feels when an author invites us to suspend our disbelief).

While the hiss of King's undead cat is an impossible terror to sustain in the foreground of our rational imaginations, it is the epitome of communicative potential. The plot cannot move forward until Louis Creed responds to the desperation of that reaction. Readers can verily weigh their responses to these horrors in tandem and, in the process, understand how someone like King or Otsuichi mines a tradition while luxuriating in the persistence of individual pets who transcend their domestication.

In each of these stories, anyone who ignores those bits and pieces activated from within behaves desperately for the same reason Louis buries his wife even after the failures of his cat and son: To admit defeat means depriving yourself of a safety screen that has been there all your life. These are people who chase after meta-questions even as they fear them. Heroes take on those questions in spite of their fears. Their sentimentality is a recent invention—an adoption from Western models, one might say—in Japanese pet-boom literature. Without it, that feeling of doing something worthwhile rapidly fades. These narratives appear to do justice to animals but are working through defensive smokescreens against the intellectual crises of confronting animal otherness. Optional responses to that otherness boil down to unconditional love or annihilation. Spotlighting animal suffering is a sly way of reinforcing our hunger for salvation. Postanimalism moves beyond that allegiance toward animals for sake of their animality. To do so undermines the immoral value of the animal even as it reinforces the valuable immorality of the human.

Postanimalism is my offering to guide us toward analyzing human-animal relations toward conscious cultivation of productive errors. It is not that we fill in the gaps of incomplete knowledge with stories of our own design but that we fill in stories of our own design with gaps of incomplete knowledge. Just as no culture can be said to operate under one linguistic identity, marking the embodied subject by its semiosis imposes a limited framework around that subject. As cultural scholars, we're contractually bound to recognize contextual specificities. Beyond that, are we forcing humanity and animality to choose between universality and particularity? Regardless of the answer, the above analyses can be nothing more than prostheses highlighting my own inability to solidify a standard of integration. In the words of Jean-Christophe Bailly (2011, 4): "The truth is that a point of solitude is always reached in one's relations with animals. When this point extends into a line and the line extends into an arch, a shelter takes shape, the very place where that solitude responds freely to its counterpart: a beloved animal." Productive error encourages us to avoid prideful traps of solitude, instead building bridges of empathetic brokenness.

Sharing traumas of any kind might not seem like a comfortable way to spend our time as pet owners and animal lovers, let alone scholars, but doing so builds us up far more equitably than sharing the triumphs we seek in denial of brokenness. Postanimalism is not a wave of the future but the whiff of a parallel reality in which agency is no longer a dirty word, regardless of the body it calls home. Like the android, Keiji, who opened this book, postanimalism reminds us that to deny the potential for life is to deny a love of death. This has nothing to do with being morbid and everything to do with falling head over heels for entropy. When Tanizaki Jun'ichirō wrote his famous essay "In Praise of Shadows," he was not simply describing what he saw to be a Western disdain for the withered and a Japanese adoration for the faded and the subtle but, more importantly, articulating the liminal boundaries between gazes and objects, breath and stone. He was, perhaps without even knowing it, also pointing toward the fuzzy distinctions between humans and animals. Without their overlapping territories, we might never get close enough to detect the piquancy of an alternative in their breath.

None of what I have written here is meant to dictate that an awareness of productive error is "required" for any of us to gain something of importance from these or any other narratives I might have included in these pages. To assert as much would be an *un*productive error in and of itself. I only wish to float it as a strategy for those to whom it might feel worthwhile among the countless other options we might pack in our intellectual toolkits. I invite anyone reading this to refine or refute what I have put forth so that we may lead each other to a dialogic understanding of epistemology from whichever disciplinary camp we choose to inhabit. Let this be not a pronouncement but a handshake.

Tyran Grillo
Summer 2023

References

Abram, David. 2010. *Becoming Animal: An Earthly Cosmology*. New York: Pantheon Books.

Alaimo, Stacy. 2010. *Bodily Natures: Science, Environment, and the Material Self*. Bloomington: Indiana University Press.

Ambros, Barbara R. 2012. *Bones of Contention: Animals and Religion in Contemporary Japan*. Honolulu: University of Hawai'i Press.

Arch, Jakobina K. 2018. *Bringing Whales Ashore: Oceans and the Environment of Early Modern Japan*. Seattle: University of Washington Press.

Bailly, Jean-Christophe. 2011. *The Animal Side*. Translated by Catherine Porter. New York: Fordham University Press.

Bandō Masako 2009. *"Koneko-goroshi" o kataru* [On "Killing Kittens"]. Tokyo: Sofusha.

Baudrillard, Jean. 2001. *Impossible Exchange*. Translated by Chris Turner. London: Verso.

——. 2008. "The Evil Demon of Images." Translated by Paul Patton and Paul Foss. In *The Jean Baudrillard Reader*, edited by Steve Redhead, 83–98. New York: Columbia University Press.

Beichman, Janine. 1986. *Masaoka Shiki*. Tokyo: Kodansha.

Berger, John. 1980. *About Looking*. New York: Pantheon Books.

Berman, Michael. 2008. "Images of Absence in P. K. Dick's *Do Androids Dream of Electric Sheep?*" In *The Everyday Fantastic: Essays on Science Fiction and Human Being*, edited by Michael Berman, 114–30. Newcastle, UK: Cambridge Scholars Publishing.

Braidotti, Rosi. 2013. *The Posthuman*. Cambridge: Polity Press.

Broglio, Ron. 2012. "Incidents in the Animal Revolution. In *Beyond Human: From Animality to Transhumanism*, edited by Charlie Blake, Claire Molloy, and Steven Shakespeare, 13–30. London: Continuum, 2012.

Butler, Judith. 2004. *Precious Life: The Powers of Mourning and Violence*. London: Verso.

Calarco, Matthew. 2008. *Zoographies: The Question of the Animal from Heidegger to Derrida*. New York: Columbia University Press.

Cassegård, Carl. 2014. *Youth Movements, Trauma and Alternative Space in Contemporary Japan*. Leiden: Global Oriental.

Castle, Gregory. 2013. *The Literary Theory Handbook*. Hoboken, NJ: John Wiley.

Cavalieri, Paola. 2009. *The Death of the Animal: A Dialogue*. New York: Columbia University Press.

Cheung, Tobias. 2010. *Transitions and Borders between Animals, Humans, and Machines, 1600–1800*. Leiden: Brill.

Coole, Diana, and Samantha Frost. 2010. "Introducing the New Materialisms." In *New Materialisms: Ontology, Agency, and Politics*, edited by Diana Coole and Samantha Frost, 1–43. Durham, NC: Duke University Press.

Creed, Barbara. 2009. *Darwin's Secrets: Evolutionary Aesthetics, Time and Sexual Display in the Cinema*. Victoria, Australia: Melbourne University Press.

Crossley, Ceri. 2004. "Anglophobia and Anti-Semitism: The Case of Alphonse Toussenel (1803–1885)." *Modern & Contemporary France* 12, no. 4: 459–72.

Csicsery-Ronay, Istvan, Jr. 2003. "Marxist Theory and Science Fiction." In *The Cambridge Companion to Science Fiction*, edited by Edward James and Farah Mendlesohn, 113–24. Cambridge: Cambridge University Press.

——. 2008. *The Seven Beauties of Science Fiction*. Middletown, CT: Wesleyan University Press.

——. "Animals and Aliens: The Emergence of the Vampire Squid from Hell." Talk given at Cornell University, September 18, 2014.

Darwin, Charles. 1876. *The Descent of Man and Selection in Relation to Sex*. New York: D. Appleton and Company.

del Caro, Adrian. 2004. *Grounding the Nietzsche Rhetoric of Earth*. Berlin: Walter de Gruyter.

Deleuze, Gilles, and Felix Guattari. 1987. *A Thousand Plateaus: Capitalism and Schizophrenia*. Translated by Brian Massumi. Minneapolis: University of Minnesota Press.

Derrida, Jacques. 2008. *The Animal That Therefore I Am*. Translated by David Wills. New York: Fordham University Press.

Dick, Philip K. 1996. *Do Androids Dream of Electric Sheep?* New York: Del Rey.

Fellenz, Marc R. 2007. *The Moral Menagerie: Philosophy and Animal Rights*. Urbana: University of Illinois Press.

Foucault, Michel. 1988. *Madness and Civilization: A History of Insanity in the Age of Reason*. Translated by Richard Howard. New York: Vintage Books.

——. 1990. *The History of Sexuality*. Volume 1, *An Introduction*. Translated by Robert Hurley. New York: Vintage.

Fujii Seiji. 2014. "'Hito o koroshite mitakatta' shōnen ga okoshita 'taiken' satsujin jiken o juzai shita mono to shite, ima omou koto" [What I think now as the one who gathered information on the murder case of the boy who "wanted to try killing someone" as an "experiment"]. *Yahoo! News Japan*. http://bylines.news.yahoo.co.jp/fujiiseiji/20140804-00037967/ (accessed January 12, 2015).

Giffney, Noreen, and Myra J. Hird. 2008. "Introduction: Queering the Non/Human." In *Queering the Non/Human (Queer Interventions)*, edited by Noreen Giffney and Myra J. Hird, 1–16. Burlington, VT: Ashgate Publishing Company.

Gledhill, Christine. 1999. "Recent Developments in Feminist Film Criticism." In *Film Theory and Criticism: Introductory Readings*, edited by Leo Braudy and Marshall Cohen, 251–72. New York: Oxford University Press.

Groemer, Gerald. 2001. "The Guild of the Blind in Tokugawa Japan." *Monumenta Nipponica* 56, no. 3: 349–80.

Gunji Nanae. 2002. *Beruna no shippo* [Berna's Tail]. Tokyo: Kadokawa Bunko.

Hallie, Philip P. 1997. "A New Kind of Rescue." In *Resisters, Rescuers, and Refugees: Historical and Ethical Issues*, edited by John J. Michalczyk, 234–37. Kansas City, MO: Sheed & Ward.

Haraway, Donna. 1994. "A Manifesto for Cyborgs: Science, Technology, and Socialist Feminism in the 1980s." In *The Postmodern Twin: New Perspectives on Social Theory*, edited by Steven Seidman, 82–115. Cambridge: Cambridge University Press.

——. 2004. *The Haraway Reader*. New York: Routledge.

——. 2008. *When Species Meet*. Minneapolis: University of Minnesota Press.

—— 2011. "Cyborgs, Coyotes and Dogs: A Kinship of Feminist Figurations." In *The New Media and Technocultures Reader*, edited by Seth Giddings and Martin Lister, 154–63. London: Routledge.

Hayashi, Reiko, and Masako Okuhiro. 2009. "The Disability-Rights Movement in Japan: Past, Present and Future." *Disability and Society: A Reader*, edited by Renu Addlakha, Stuart Blume, Patrick Devlieger, Osamu Nagase, and Myriam Winance, 391–410. New Delhi: Orient Blackswan.

Hayles, Katherine. 1999. *How We Became Posthuman: Virtual Bodies in Cybernetics, Literature, and Informatics*. Chicago: University of Chicago Press.

Hearne, Vicki. 1994. *Animal Happiness*. New York: Harper Collins.

Heidegger, Martin. 1996. *Hölderlin's Hymn "The Ister."* Translated by William McNeill and Julia Davis. Bloomington: Indiana University Press.

—— 2000. "Hölderlin and the Essence of Poetry." In *Elucidations of Hölderlin's Poetry*, translated by Keith Hoeller, 51–65. Amherst, NY: Humanity Books.

Heinrich, Bernd. 2012. *Life Everlasting: The Animal Way of Death*. Boston: Houghton Mifflin Harcourt.

Hendershot, Cynthia. 1999. *Paranoia, the Bomb, and 1950s Science Fiction Films*. Bowling Green, OH: Bowling Green State University Popular Press.

Herman, Judith. 1992. *Trauma and Recovery: The Aftermath of Violence—from Domestic Abuse to Political Terror*. New York: Basic Books.

Hiller, Anne E. 2015. "Dystopia 101: The Millennials React to *Metropolis*." In *Apocalyptic Projections: A Study of Past Predictions, Current Trends and Future Intimations as Related to Film and Literature*, edited by Annette M. Magid, 80–109. Newcastle upon Tyne, UK: Cambridge Scholars Publishing.

Holt, Jon. 2016. "Literature Short on Time: Modern Moments in Haiku and Tanka." In *Routledge Handbook of Modern Japanese Literature*, edited by Rachael Hutchinson and Leith Morton, 26–41. London: Routledge.

Innes, C. D. 1998. *Edward Gordon Craig: A Vision of the Theatre*. Amsterdam: Harwood Academic Publishers.

Inokuma Hisashi. 2001. "Kore kara no inugaku: hito to no yoriyoi kankei o motomete" [The Future of Cynology: Toward a Better Relationship with Humans]. In *Inu no dōbutsugaku* [Zoology of the Domestic Dog], edited by Hayashi Yoshihiro and Satō Hideaki, 151–68. Tokyo: University of Tokyo Press.

Inudō Isshin. 2013. "Komento" [Comments]. Last modified June 5. http://inunekoningen2.com/comments.

Ishida Osamu. 2008. *Gendai Nihonjin no dōbutsukan* [Modern Japanese Perceptions of Animals]. Tokyo: Being Net Press.

Ishiguro Kengo. 2001. *Mōdōken Kuiiru no isshō* [Quill: The Life of a Guide Dog]. Tokyo: Bungei Shunjū.

———. 2003. *Kuiiru e no tegami* [Letters to Quill]. Tokyo: Bungei Shunjū.

Itoh, Mayumi. 2010. *Japanese Wartime Zoo Policy: The Silent Victims of World War II.* New York: Palgrave Macmillan.

Iwakuma, Miho. 2001. "Ageing with Disability in Japan." In *Disability and the Life Course: Global Perspectives*, edited by Mark Priestly, 219–30. Cambridge: Cambridge University Press.

Jeong, Seung-hoon. 2011. "Animals: An Adventure in Bazin's Ontology." In *Opening Bazin: Postwar Film Theory and Its Afterlife*, edited by Dudley Andrew and Hervé Joubert-Laurencin, 177–85. Oxford: Oxford University Press.

jones, pattrice. 2007. *Aftershock: Confronting Trauma in a Violent World: A Guide for Activists and Their Allies.* New York: Lantern Books.

Kambayashi Chōhei. 2004. *Hadae no shita* [Under the Skin]. Volume 1. Tokyo: Hayakawa Bunko.

Karatani Kōjin. 1993. *Origins of Modern Japanese Literature.* Translated and edited by Brett de Bary. Durham, NC: Duke University Press.

Kerekes, David, and David Slater. 1995. *Killing for Culture: An Illustrated History of Death Film.* London: Creation Books.

Kete, Kathleen. 1994. *The Beast in the Boudoir: Petkeeping in Nineteenth-Century Paris.* Berkeley: University of California Press.

Kim, Eunjung. 2012. "Why Do Dolls Die? The Power of Passivity and the Embodied Interplay Between Disability and Sex Dolls." *Review of Education, Pedagogy, and Cultural Studies* 34, no. 3/4: 94–106.

King, Stephen. 1984. *Pet Sematary.* New York: Signet.

———. 2002. *Pet Sematary.* New York: Pocket Books.

Kitano Yūsaku. 2012. *Kame-kun* [Mr. Turtle]. Tokyo: Kawade Shobō Shinsha.

———. 2016. *Mr. Turtle.* Translated by Tyran Grillo. Fukuoka, Japan: Kurodahan Press.

Knight, John. 2003. *Waiting for Wolves in Japan: An Anthropological Study of People-Wildlife Relations.* Oxford: Oxford University Press.

———. 2011. *Herding Monkeys to Paradise: How Macaque Troops are Managed for Tourism in Japan.* Leiden: Brill.

Kobayashi Teruyuki. 2006. *Doriimu bokkusu: Korosareteyuku petto-tachi* [Dream Boxes: The Ongoing Killing of Pets]. Tokyo: Mainichi Shimbun-sha.

Kogan, Vivian. 2006. *The "I" of History: Self-Fashioning and National Consciousness in Jules Michelet.* Chapel Hill: University of North Carolina Department of Romance Languages.

LaMarre, Thomas. 2008. "Speciesism, Part I: Translating Races into Animals." *Mechademia Second Arc* 3, no. 1: 75–95.

Lane, John. 2007. *Circling Home.* Athens: University of Georgia Press.

Latour, Bruno. 2005. *Reassembling the Social: An Introduction to Actor-Network-Theory.* Oxford: Oxford University Press.

Laycock, Stephen W. 1999. "The Animal *as* Animal: A Plea for Open Conceptuality." In *Animal Others: On Ethics, Ontology, and Animal Life*, edited by H. Peter Steeves, 271–84. Albany: SUNY Press.

Lippit, Akira Mizuta. 2000. *Electric Animal: Toward a Rhetoric of Wildlife*. Minneapolis: University of Minnesota Press.

Lippit, Noriko Mizuta. 1999. "Poe in Japan." In *Poe Abroad: Influences and Affinities*, edited by Lois Davis Vines, 135–48. Iowa City: University of Iowa Press.

Liu, Petrus. 2012. "Queer Human Rights in and against China: Marxism and the Figuration of the Human." *Social Text* 30, no. 1: 71–89.

Livingston, Julie, and Jasbir Puar. 2011. "Introduction." *Social Text "Interspecies" Special Issue* 29, no. 1: 3–14.

Marran, Christine L. 2017. *Ecology without Culture: Aesthetics for a Toxic World*. Minneapolis: University of Minnesota Press.

Maruyama, Masao. 1965. "Patterns of Individuation and the Case of Japan: A Conceptual Scheme." In *Changing Japanese Attitudes toward Modernization*, edited by Marius B. Jansen, 489–531. Princeton, NJ: Princeton University Press.

Marx, Karl, and Frederick Engels. 2005. *The Communist Manifesto: A Road Map to History's most Important Political Document*, edited by Phil Gasper. Chicago: Haymarket Books.

Marx, Karl. 2009. "Estranged Labour." *Economic and Philosophical Manuscripts of 1844*. Last modified September 23. https://www.marxists.org/archive/marx/works/1844/manuscripts/labour.htm.

——. 2020. "On *The Jewish Question*." *Works of Karl Marx 1844*. Last modified May 19. https://www.marxists.org/archive/marx/works/1844/jewish-question/.

Matsunaka, Kumiko, and Naoko Koda. 2008. "Acceptance of Dog Guides and Daily Stress Levels of Dog Guide Users and Nonusers." *Journal of Visual Impairment & Blindness* 102, no. 5: 295–304.

Mazis, Glen A. 2008. *Humans, Animals, Machines: Blurring Boundaries*. Albany: SUNY Press.

Mbembe, Achille. 2008. "Necropolitics." In *Foucault in an Age of Terror: Essays on Biopolitics and the Defence of Society*, edited by Stephen Morton and Stephen Bygrave, 152–82. New York: Palgrave Macmillan.

McHugh, Susan. 2011. *Animal Stories: Narrating across Species Lines*. Minneapolis: University of Minnesota Press.

McKee, Daniel. 2007. "Letting the Beasts Do the Talking: Animal Motifs and Japanese Paintings as Statements of Personal and Social Identity." In *A Brush with Animals: Japanese Paintings 1700–1950*, edited by Robert Schaap and Willem R. van Gulik, 9–18. Bergejik, Netherlands: Society of Japanese Arts.

Michalko, Rod. 1998. *The Mystery of the Eye and the Shadow of Blindness*. Toronto: University of Toronto Press.

Miles, Michael. 2000. "Disability on a Different Model: Glimpses of an Asian Heritage." *Disability & Society* 15, no. 4: 603–18.

Millan, Cesar, with Melissa Jo Peltier. 2006. *Cesar's Way: The Natural, Everyday Guide to Understanding and Correcting Common Dog Problems*. New York: Harmony Books.

Miller, Harlan B. 2009. "No Escape." In *The Death of the Animal: A Dialogue*, edited by Paola Cavalieri, 59–71. New York: Columbia University Press.

Miller, Ian. 2005. "Didactic Nature: Exhibiting Nation and Empire at the Ueno Zoological Gardens." In *JAPANimals: History and Culture in Japan's Animal Life*, edited by Gregory M. Pflugfelder and Brett L. Walker, 273–314. Ann Arbor: The University of Michigan Center for Japanese Studies.

———. 2013. *The Nature of the Beasts: Empire and Exhibition at the Tokyo Imperial Zoo.* Berkeley: University of California Press.

Miller, Sam. 2011. "The Limits of Language." In *Eiko & Koma: Time Is Not Even, Space Is Not Empty*, edited by Joan Rothfuss, 282–87. Minneapolis: Walker Art Center.

Milton, Kay. 2005. "Anthropomorphism or Egomorphism? The Perception of Non-Human Persons by Human Ones." In *Animals in Person: Cultural Perspectives on Human-Animal Intimacy*, edited by John Knight, 231–71. Oxford: Berg.

Mitchell, David T., and Sharon L. Snyder. 2000. *Narrative Prosthesis: Disability and the Dependencies of Discourse.* Ann Arbor: University of Michigan Press.

Møller, Lis. 1991. *The Freudian Reading: Analytical and Fictional Constructions.* Philadelphia: University of Pennsylvania Press.

Monroe, Kristen Renwick. 1996. *The Heart of Altruism: Perceptions of a Common Humanity.* Princeton, NJ: Princeton University Press.

Moulthrop, Stuart, and Dene Grigar. 2017. *Traversals: The Use of Preservation for Early Electronic Writing.* Cambridge, MA: MIT Press.

Mulhall, Stephen. 2009. *The Wounded Animal: J. M. Coetzee and the Difficulty of Reality in Literature and Philosophy.* Princeton, NJ: Princeton University Press.

Mulvey, Laura. 1988. "Visual Pleasure and Narrative Cinema." In *Feminism and Film Theory*, edited by Constance Penley, 57–68. New York: Routledge.

Murakami, Fuminobu. 1996. *Ideology and Narrative in Modern Japan Literature.* Assen, Netherlands: Van Gorcum.

Nakamura Ikuo. 2010. *Nihonjin no shūkyō to dōbutsukan: Sesshō to nikushoku* [Japanese Religion and Perceptions of Animals: Killing and Meat Consumption]. Tokyo: Yoshikawa Kobunkan.

Nietzsche, Friedrich. 1996. *Human, All Too Human: A Book for Free Spirits.* Translated by Marion Faber and Stephen Lehmann. Lincoln: University of Nebraska Press.

Nussbaum, Martha C. 2006. *Frontiers of Justice: Disability, Nationality, Species Membership.* Cambridge, MA: Belknap Press.

Nye, David E. 1994. *American Technological Sublime.* Cambridge, MA: MIT Press.

Oakes, David A. 2000. *Science and Destabilization in the Modern American Gothic: Lovecraft, Matheson, and King.* Westport, CT: Greenwood Press.

Oberst, Joachim L. 2009. *Heidegger on Language and Death: The Intrinsic Connection in Human Existence.* London: Continuum.

Ōe Kenzaburō. 1996. *Hiroshima Notes.* Translated by David L. Swain and Toshi Yonezawa. New York: Grove Press.

Oliner, Samuel P., and Pearl M. Oliner. 1988. *The Altruistic Personality: Rescuers of Jews in Nazi Europe.* New York: Free Press.

Olmert, Meg Daley. 2009. *Made for Each Other: The Biology of the Human-Animal Bond.* Cambridge, MA: Lifelong Books.

Ōmura Eishō. 2009. "Shōshi kōreika shakai no naka no petto—petto to neo famirizumu" [Pets in a Society of Declining Birth Rates and Aging Population: Pets and Neo-Familism]. In *Petto to shakai* [Pets and Society], edited by Mori Yūji and Okuno Takuji, 131–54. Tokyo: Iwanami Shoten.

Ōno Tomoya. 1988. *Shōgaisha wa, ima* [The Disabled, as of Now]. Tokyo: Iwanami Shinsho.

Ototake Hirotada. 2000. *No One's Perfect*. Translated by Gerry Harcourt. Tokyo: Kodansha International.

Otsuichi. 2003. *Heimen inu* [Flat Dog]. Tokyo: Shūeisha.

Overboe, James. 2012. "Theory, Impairment and Impersonal Singularities: Deleuze, Guattari and Agamben." In *Disability and Social Theory: New Developments and Directions*, edited by Dan Goodley, Bill Hughes, and Lennard Davis, 112–26. New York: Palgrave Macmillan.

Pedersen, Helena. 2011. "Release the Moths: Critical Animal Studies and the Posthumanist Impulse." *Culture, Theory and Critique* 52, no. 1: 65–81.

Pettman, Dominic. 2011. *Human Error: Species-Being and Media Machines*. Minneapolis: University of Minnesota Press.

Pierce, Jessica. 2012. *The Last Walk: Reflections on Our Pets at the End of Their Lives*. Chicago: University of Chicago Press.

Plourde, Lorraine. 2014. "Cat Cafés, Affective Labor, and the Healing Boom in Japan." *Japanese Studies* 34, no. 2: 115–33.

Pollard, Bill. 2003. "Can Virtuous Actions be Both Habitual and Rational?" *Ethical Theory and Moral Practice* 6: 411–25.

Proctor, Robert N., and Londa Schiebinger, eds. 2008. *Agnotology: The Making and Unmaking of Ignorance*. Stanford, CA: Stanford University Press.

Rees, Clea F., and Jonathan Webber. 2014. "Automaticity in Virtuous Action." In *The Philosophy and Psychology of Character and Happiness*, edited by Nancy E. Snow and Franco V. Trivigno, 75–90. New York: Routledge.

Richie, Donald. 2001. *A Hundred Years of Japanese Film: A Concise History, with a Selective Guide to Video and DVDs*. New York: Kodansha International.

Sas, Miryam. 2011. *Experimental Arts in Postwar Japan: Moments of Encounter, Engagement, and Imagined Return*. Cambridge, MA: Harvard University Press.

Sasabe Yōichirō. 2001. "Chosha intabyū: Kitano Yūsaku" [Author Interview: Kitano Yūsaku]. http://www.sf-fantasy.com/magazine/interview/010302.shtml.

Sasaki Yuri. 2007. *Shōgaiken Tarō no maichini* [Day by Day with Tarō, the Disabled Dog]. Tokyo: Aspect.

Seed, David. 2011. *Science Fiction: A Very Short Introduction*. Oxford: Oxford University Press.

Shaviro, Steven. 2015. *Discognition*. London: Repeater.

Shaw, Bruce. 2010. *The Animal Fable in Science Fiction and Fantasy*. Jefferson, NC: McFarland & Company.

Shukin, Nicole. 2009. *Animal Capital: Rendering Life in Biopolitical Times*. Minneapolis: University of Minnesota Press.

Siebers, Tobin. 2011. *Disability Theory*. Ann Arbor: University of Michigan Press.

Silvers, Anita. 2010. "An Essay on Modeling: The Social Model of Disability." In *Philosophical Reflections on Disability*, edited by D. Christopher Ralston and Justin Ho, 19–36. New York: Springer.

Singer, Peter. 1990. *Animal Liberation*. New York: New York Review Books.

Skabelund, Aaron. 2011. *Empire of Dogs: Canines, Japan, and the Making of the Modern Imperial World*. Ithaca, NY: Cornell University Press.

Snaza, Nathan. 2015. "Toward a Geneaology of Educational Humanism." In *Posthumanism and Educational Research*, edited by Nathan Snaza and John A. Weaver, 17–29. New York: Routledge.

Stapledon, Olaf. 2011. *Sirius*. London: Gollancz.

Stevens, Carolyn S. 2013. *Disability in Japan*. London: Routledge.

Stiker, Henri-Jacques. 1999. *A History of Disability*. Translated by William Sayers. Ann Arbor: University of Michigan Press.

Suvin, Darko. 1979. *Metamorphoses of Science Fiction: On the Poetics and History of a Literary Genre*. New Haven: Yale University Press.

Swabe, Joanna. 2005. "Loved to Death? Veterinary Visions of Pet-keeping in Modern Dutch Society." In *Animals in Person: Cultural Perspectives on Human-Animal Intimacy*, edited by John Knight, 101–18. Oxford: Berg.

Takashina, Shuji. 1990. "Natsume Sōseki and the Development of Modern Japanese Art." In *Culture and Identity: Japanese Intellectuals during the Interwar Years*, edited by J. Thomas Rimer, 273–81. Princeton, NJ: Princeton University Press.

Taleb, Nassim Nicholas. 2014. *Antifragile: Things That Gain from Disorder*. New York: Random House.

Tatsumi, Takayuki. 2006. *Full Metal Apache: Transactions between Cyberpunk Japan and Avant-Pop America*. Durham, NC: Duke University Press.

Thomson, Rosemarie Garland. 1997. *Extraordinary Bodies: Figuring Physical Disability in American Culture and Literature*. New York: Columbia University Press.

Thurtle, Phillip, and Robert Mitchell. 2004. "Data Made Flesh: The Material Poiesis of Informatics." In *Data Made Flesh: Embodying Information*, edited by Robert Mitchell and Phillip Thurtle, 1–26. New York: Routledge.

Titchkosky, Tanya, and Rod Michalko. 2012. "The Body as the Problem of Individuality: A Phenomenological Disability Studies Approach." In *Disability and Social Theory: New Developments and Directions*, edited by Dan Goodley, Bill Hughes, and Lennard Davis, 127–42. New York: Palgrave Macmillan.

Tran, Jonathan. 2011. *Foucault and Theology*. London: T&T Clark International.

Tremain, Shelley, ed. 2005. *Foucault and the Government of Disability*. Ann Arbor: University of Michigan Press.

Tuan, Yi-Fu. 1984. *Dominance & Affection: The Making of Pets*. New Haven: Yale University Press.

Ueda, Makoto. 1976. *Modern Japanese Writers and the Nature of Literature*. Stanford, CA: Stanford University Press.

Ueno Chizuko. 1994. *Kindai kazoku no seiritsu to shūen* [The Rise and Fall of the Modern Family]. Tokyo: Iwanami Shoten.

Uexküll, Jakob von. 2001. "An Introduction to Umwelt." *Semiotica* 134: 107–110.

Victor, Elizabeth [Eloise and Rusty]. 2011. *Smart Paws: Ancient Partner to Service Dog Today*. Bloomington, IN: iUniverse.

Vint, Sherryl. 2009. "Species and Species-Being: Alienated Subjectivity and the Commodification of Animals." In *Red Planets: Marxism and Science Fiction*, edited by Mark Bould and China Miéville, 118–36. Middletown, CT: Wesleyan University Press.

——. 2016. "The Biopolitics of Globalization in Damir Lukacevic's *Transfer*." In *Red Alert: Marxist Approaches to Science Fiction Cinema*, edited by Ewa Mazierska and Alfred Suppia, 98–120. Detroit: Wayne State University Press.

Waal, Frans de. 1996. *Good Natured: The Origins of Right and Wrong in Humans and Other Animals*. Cambridge, MA: Harvard University Press.

Wada-Marciano, Mitsuyo. 2009. "The Postwar Japanese Melodrama." Translated by Bianca Briciu. *Review of Japanese Culture and Society* 21: 19–32.

Walker, Brett L. 2005a. "Introduction." In *JAPANimals: History and Culture in Japan's Animal Life*, edited by Gregory M. Pflugfelder and Brett L. Walker, 1–20. Ann Arbor: The University of Michigan Center for Japanese Studies.

——. 2005b. *The Lost Wolves of Japan*. Seattle: University of Washington Press.

Weinstone, Anne. 2004. *Avatar Bodies: A Tantra for Posthumanism*. Minneapolis: University of Minnesota Press.

Whyte, Susan Reynolds, and Herbert Muyinda. 2007. "Wheels and New Legs: Mobilization in Uganda." In *Disability in Local and Global Worlds*, edited by Benedicte Ingstad and Susan Reynolds Whyte, 287–310. Berkeley: University of California Press.

Williams, Linda. 1984. "'Something Else Besides a Mother': *Stella Dallas* and the Maternal Melodrama." *Journal of Cinema and Media Studies* 24, no. 1: 2–27.

Wolfe, Cary. 2008. "Learning from Temple Grandin, or, Animal Studies, Disability Studies, and Who Comes after the Subject." *New Formations* 64: 110–25.

——. 2010. *What Is Posthumanism?* Minneapolis: University of Minnesota Press.

Yamashita Tsuneo. 1984. *Sabetsu no shinteki sekai* [The Mental World of Discrimination]. Tokyo: Gendai Shokan.

Yoshimoto, Mitsuhiro. 1993. "Melodrama, Postmodernism, and Japanese Cinema." In *Melodrama and Asian Cinema*, edited by Wimal Dissanayake, 101–26. Cambridge: Cambridge University Press.

Zhong, Wenwen. 2011. "Modern Guide Dog Movement in Japan: Elites, Visually Impaired Persons and the General Public." Master's thesis, Lund University.

www.ingramcontent.com/pod-product-compliance
Lightning Source LLC
Chambersburg PA
CBHW031119020726
47495CB00007B/2263